William Caswell Jones

Birch-Rod Days

And Other Poems

William Caswell Jones

Birch-Rod Days
And Other Poems

ISBN/EAN: 9783744705202

Printed in Europe, USA, Canada, Australia, Japan

Cover: Foto ©Thomas Meinert / pixelio.de

More available books at **www.hansebooks.com**

BIRCH-ROD DAYS

AND

OTHER POEMS.

BY

WILLIAM C. JONES.

CHICAGO:
AMERICAN PUBLISHERS' ASSOCIATION.
1892.

MARY — MY PLAYMATE WHEN A CHILD;

THE IDOL OF MY BOYHOOD — WILD;

THE DEAREST WIFE OF MANHOOD DAYS —

I WILL TO THEE INSCRIBE MY LAYS.

THE WATER LILY.

Rippling rills that run down to the sea,
    Are but tears which the winter has shed;
When the Flower-Angel melts them all free
    And her cold, chilly ice-chains have fled.

If the stars be the flowers of the heaven!
    Then the flowers are the stars of the earth;
Which God in compassion has given —
    To us priceless for beauty and worth.

We garland the bride of the morrow
    With the fairest and loveliest bloom;
We place them in wreaths in our sorrow
    When the coffin is laid in the tomb.

A joy to the sad ones left weeping;
    An emblem of the rich golden-dawn;
Of spring-time the Father is keeping
    In heaven where the loved ones have gone.

"Take this," and most sacredly guard it,
    It is Truth's germ, I give to your clan;

From the Flower-Angel ever regard it
   A rare bulb that is priceless to man!

A bloom 'twill in beauty glow ever,
   Resplendent in the sunshine or rain,
'Twill free thee of vice — from sin sever —
   Truth I give thee to always maintain.

A slave to base passions, and in crime,
   Man trod Truth prostrate under his feet;
In the marshes, in filth, and in slime
   Her destruction and loss seemed complete.

Winter drew near with her tears all chilled;
   Her storms raging on seas, and the lands;
Rains beat down and the marshes were filled,
   And ice-fettered by her cold, cold hands.

And God smote man for his sin and lust;
   And for his struggle for worldly power;
Not willing to love or Him to trust
   Until the final and fatal hour.

A window in heaven is open thrown,
   And the Flower-Angel breathes upon earth;
All nature smiles, and the valleys groan —
   Teeming in beauty, and lovely birth.

THE WATER LILY.

The valleys rejoice; the rocks laugh loud;
    While the green-covered trees clap their
        hands;
The hills sing out; and the mountains proud
    Echo the refrain over the lands.

The waters wide now cover the place
    Of brutish man's sad and reckless ruth;
Where once he had trampled in disgrace
    The Flower-Angel's bulb, the germ of Truth.

A maiden came there with her lover fair,
    And she launched her light boat on the deep;
In sailing around espied what were
    Twelve spotless white flowers quite fast
        asleep.

The maid bent low at the lovely scene,
    Then touching the fairest of the flowers,
"Why not, fair sister, O water queen,
    Join us in this fairy-land of ours?"

"Dearest maiden, I'm thy sister Truth,
    Whom the Flower-Angel gave away
Unto a man in his reckless youth,
    With whom I loved and I longed to stay.

"But he crushed me, and I bleeding died,
    And was buried in the marshes low;
Where the Flower-Angel came and me espied,
    Then soon again I began to grow.

"Luxuriant leaves of the richest green,
    And lovely white flowers, spotless and pure;
Crown now my head as the water-queen,
    O'er the deep disgrace I couldn't endure."

And the maiden bent low her head once more:
    "Thy name shall be Lily," she softly said;
"White Water-Lily Truth, I adore,
    Purest, and fairest, raise up thy head!"

The Lily said, "There's not a stain,
    Though bitter my hours in life now past,
'Truth crushed to earth shall rise again,'
    Be true to herself until the last."

The Lily shall be an emblem pure
    Of virtue, beauty, and lovely grace;
And woman's love will ever endure
    In the heart of man to hold first place.

CONTENTS.

PROEM: The Water Lily.

A Charivari	150
A Guest of the Club	132
Allie	179
A Merciless Mind	131
An Episode	175
An Ill-Formed Alliance	219
An Ill-Sorted League	217
Autumn Leaves	101
Avarice	119
Best Look Before You Leap	165
Better Than Gold	77
Birch-Rod Days	17
Caution	153
Changes	187
Christmas	215
Coins	235
Crafty	212
Cupid and Death	92
Dame Fortune	117
Daunt Not the Spirit	191
Deception	221
Discontent	155
Discretion	201
Dissension	205
Drones vs. Bees	115

CONTENTS.

Fail Not	91
Flattery	161
Forgive, O That Religion	193
Friendship's Disease	87
Help	167
Hypocrisy	172
Idle-whiles	79
Idly-Heeding	123
In Contempt	159
In Fancy Dreaming	71
Integrity	163
Keats	47
Labor has Its Reward	157
Life's Grapes	224
Lingering at the Grave	52
Little Lights	39
Little Physician	180
Love's Arrows	69
Luxury and Ease	176
Madie Green	102
Mine, Only Mine	99
Mocking-bird and Jay	88
Molliter Manus Imposuit	169
My Florida	51
My Lady Fair	207
My Loves	233
My Mary	185
Old Age	72
Oppression	231
Our Country Home	75
Our Faithful Servants	125

CONTENTS.   iii

Polly, You Talk Too Much	143
Recompense	149
Rejected	90
Scotch Letter	209
Sic Iter Ad Astra	64
Sleep and Hope	105
Spare the Rod and Spoil the Child	129
Summer's Labor	203
Sunny Southern Home	97
Sweet Lady, I Love Thy Fair Face	96
Temporal Power	195
The Battle-Flag	83
The Cross Ill-Natured Man	60
The Dancing Kid	127
The Disastrous Crossing	147
The Farmer's Soliloquy	173
The Felon's Dream	94
The Felon's Soliloquy	43
The Fireside	213
The Harvest of Death	40
The Man of Dignity	139
The Miser	225
The Mocking-bird	48
The Orator	63
The Relation of Man to Nature	239
The Reward of Stealth	229
The Smile of Woman	145
The Templar	85
The Thrush	121
The Train	55
The Traitor Bird	108

The Tree and the Rose	58
The Twilight Shades	81
The Wabash	111
The World is Cold and Dreary	109
Three Plagues	189
To Mary	194
To My Wife	73
To Portia	190
Transformation	137
Treacherous Friendship	232
True Might	199
Union is Strength	122
Valor	141
What Is Fame?	67
What Is Life?	183
What Is There Better Man Can Do?	197
When Fortune Frowns	45
Who May Serve Well?	113

BIRCH-ROD DAYS

AND OTHER POEMS.

BIRCH-ROD DAYS.

Fond memory still recalls the day
Of tyrannizing birch-rod sway,
When sturdy teacher, of the old-time school,
Did govern well with rod and rule.
His unrelenting look, his solemn mien,
May, in imagination, still be seen;
And the truant, disobedient of his law,
Recalls how quick he was to find some flaw;
Remembers youthful days — the days of woe —
When oft was dealt the unforgiving blow
Upon the back, oft minus coat and vest,
Of hapless youth, for trifles, thus opprest.

Who dared to look or feel a moment gay,
Felt his coercion all that day!

Well calculated to suppress all noise,
His laws inexorable —were for boys.
We would rebel, yet each rebellious time
Were scored with the birch-rod, as for some crime.
Forgive him! Never! My heart revolting swells
With wicked thoughts, when back my memory dwells.
Yet, I remember, when in days now past,
We were all taught to spell, alike and fast;
To syllable and pronounce were taught it well—
Taught from the spelling book—learned how to spell;
The class in reading, from books, were taught to read.
The teacher had one purpose—to succeed;
And grammar, boys and girls were sparse
Who could not give the well-known rules and parse;
Each winter brought us to the rule of three,
And we could cipher well—for well could he;
In writing the teacher would oft indite
This couplet, in our home-made copy-books to write:
"A man of words and not of deeds
Is like a garden full of weeds."
And well we wrote, and there was scarce a blot—
For praises from his grace quite oft were sought—

But never given, unless true worth was there—
Worth was not found, if it was, I'm not aware.
Among them all, alone there is but one
My memory loves to dwell upon;
He spared the rod on me, a helpless wight,
And made me love him, ruled me not by might;
Judge was he then, as now supreme—
Best of them all, be he alone my theme:

ACROSTIC.

Just man! A friend to my early days,
All hail, for thee can I sing praise!
Clear was thy head in discrimination then— [men;
Oft hast thou since shown it 'mong thy walks with
Brilliant in speech, sweet voiced also; [show.
When first I knew thee, thou did'st thy greatness
When in my boyhood days, young, frank and free,
In thy tuition I loved to be;
Led by thy teaching we first inclined
Knowledge to obtain for the youthful mind.
Infinite thy kind offices—we name thee—
Noblest of men—true as man can be.

As the mind recalls those days, I am proud
There is one enduring without a cloud
To darken.   Brilliant to-day — bright was then —
Best of dear teachers — loveliest of men ;
Who ruled and governed well — one always may
Kindly — without dictatorial sway.

My memory loves to dwell upon those days —
For even 'midst the clouds of mist and haze
Life's brightest sunshine will appear
When looking back o'er times we now revere.
Ah, chilling time! we turn aside to glance
And find thy fancied visions all romance ;
Thy fondest hopes, thy brightest dreams,
Sad memories for life's after themes.

We hear no more the gentle, child-like voice,
Who long, long years ago was youthful choice
Of one who bent with years, now silvered gray,
Waits but for time to bear his cares away;
Waits for the hour to come when life is o'er,
When he shall join her on the other shore.

CLARA.

I think me now of one sweet girl,
That was the gem, 'mong many a maiden pearl,
That grew in loveliness and grace
Until we loved her — time will ne'er efface
The memory of her sparkling eyes —
Bright as the stars, that nightly jewel skies;
And the wavy tresses of her dark-brown hair
Were soft and silken, as her face was fair;
Lithe was her form, each perfect part
Chiseled as 'twere for the sculptor's art;
With voice full round, so soft and sweet,
She spoke not word you would not wish repeat.
But like the wild flowers we used to gather
And bring to her from off the heather,
She too has faded. Gone now to rest
With Him who gave that angel spirit blest
Unto the friends, who lingering stay
To watch and weep o'er now her lifeless clay.
Who is there that hath not stood by the grave
Of some dear friend, and tried most brave

To stop the silent tear that trickled down with sorrow
All the fond hopes of the bright to-morrow?
Who is there that does not now recall
The sorrow of the funeral knell and pall?
Who is there here on earth who would not give
His own sweet life, one dear to him might live?
Who is there who has not felt the sting and tear
Of bitter anguish losing friends most dear?
And yet 'mongst God's angel-forms and fairies,
I'll find, I know, some day, loved Clara's!

THE SKATE.

December's sun had risen bright and clear;
Red cheeks and blue noses told winter was severe.
But boys were happy, for the chill of night
Brought to them visions of rare delight!
The creek was frozen o'er, its glistening ice
Was to their minds a part of paradise;
And morning's task at home complete,
Each buckled on his skates for winter's treat.
Alas! the glittering surface of the ice
Did many a truant boy from school entice.

The swiftest was a "deer," and soon the race,
For forty lusty throats quick gave him chase!
The school bell rang, although its notes were clear,
What cared we for it, while playing deer?
Away we went, each steady stroke
But hours of distance on us broke;
And as the race more intense grew
It seemed to each he fairly flew!
When, at last, we caught the long-chased deer,
The air was rent with deafening cheer!
It was then boys circles cut, and eagles spread —
While some cut letters that were plainly read!
On ice we ran to see who could farthest jump —
Saw stars, in daylight, as our heads would thump!
Yes, mingled we in sports, then, o'er and o'er,
Just as boys mingled in the days of yore.
Then schoolward turned, each skater gay,
Little did he list, the weal that he must pay.
The homeward journey one always tires
And passes little that he first admires;
'Tis true of life, we pass ambition's goal,
Then pray to rest the weary mind and soul.

Ah, noble youth, thy freaks are oft despised,
When better judgment would them have prized!
Think you, my friend, that boyish vim
Augurs not but usefulness to follow him?
Exultant youth, both bright and gay,
Will ever live to bear life's prize away?
Reached we at last the school-house door, our faces
 bright,
Forgetful of the hour, in our delight—
His angry looks, his sullen tones,
Were worse than next day's aching bones —
His switches? I remember—and live to tell —
How well he used them — Aye, used them well!

THE HUTSON MASSACRE.

In eighteen hundred and ten, a pioneer,
Named Hutson, left for the wilderness, then here.
His wife was with him, and six dear boys and girls;
One, a maiden of sixteen, had soft brown curls,
And bright blue eyes, with cheeks so fair,
They would with lilies well compare!
The daughter was the idol of her father's heart —

And when the time had come they must depart
For the unknown, and then far distant west,
She was with all his plans imprest.
Hardships were endured, and privations by the way
But laughed at, in hopes of a better day.
Then came they to a land in Nature's dress—
A plain and valley teeming in fruitfulness:
Earth had not then, nor now, a lovelier spot,
Than the grand old prairie of Lamotte!
It was here Hutson built a homely dwelling—
A rude log cabin — his stout heart welling
With joy o'er the happiness it gave to him,
To be thus safely housed in a cabin trim.
Time went smoothly on until the season's close,
When their harvest warned them of the savage foes!
Plundering, murdering, committing ravages,
Around that cabin home were lurking savages,
Who for the pale face had the most intense hate—
Yet none was more cruel than the Hutsons' fate:
One evening, as the sun sank in the west,
A mother sat watching, with babe at breast,
The return of father who had gone to mill

Miles of distance, across the plain and hill.
Would that lovely sunset, as it westward fell,
Could but their fate to them foretell!
Calmly she waits — when yells of Indian devils
Break now upon her — death in carnage revels!
Her babe was into a boiling caldron thrown;
Mother and children tomahawked, save one lone
Sweet girl; who was their captive led
To live a life of shame and dread!
Then to that cabin was placed a torch of fire,
The lifeless hurled thereon! While with demon's ire
They watched the rolling flames and curling smoke,
Till sighing embers, and faint glare, the end bespoke!
Hutson came home! Though strong of frame
Intensely haggard his face became!
"My wife! my children!" Then 'mid the agony
  of woe,
The teardrops from their fountain ceased to flow!
The carnage was complete. Aye, well he knew
The brutal nature of the scene in view!
Hutson, from all once near and dear, then turned,
And while on horse, as heart within him burned,

Vowed eternal vengeance, o'er and o'er,
Against the Indians evermore.
Well did he keep that vow! Week after week,
He with his trusty rifle did vengeance seek;
Until, at last, he too was known to fall
At the head of troop, pierced by the Indian's ball!
And the old creek, where we boys used to skate,
Was named Hutson, o'er his untimely fate;
And on the Wabash banks, 'bove and 'neath the hill,
Sits to his memory, the village — Hutsonville.
'Tis said that we grow old! That time's decay
Will change our feelings day by day;
That man will change the purpose of his youth,
And feel that all is fading — even truth;
That what is good lived only in the past —
The world's degenerating fast and fast.
The lawyer lays aside his book, grown old,
Which once such precious truths had told,
And folds the door upon the musty shelf,
And feels despondent with the world and self —
Then moralizes o'er his time and fate,

And blames the world, not his declining state;
But youth, exultant, with eager look,
Will gather up the shelf-worn book;
He will its pages anew read o'er,
And glean fresh treasures from its store.
He will for the future each day plan
And feel the world depends on coming man;
New cities shall grow up, the future great,
Will rival all the past in Church and State!
'Tis ever thus; the old shall weary be,
While youth is buoyant, lithe and free;
And feels the world, with all its broad expanse
Is made for him, his pleasures to enhance;
And grapples with it, new treasures sure to find,
That ever yield to his inquiring mind.
One age declines, another takes its place,
And progress ever marks our noble race.
Aye, man! no matter what thy sphere,
Thy memory loves to wander back to things once
    dear;
And dear to thee, which after years will trace,
Are all the scenes of boyhood's time and place.

Call back in memory, ye gray-haired sires,
Call back to memory your youthful fires;
Call back the laws you once transgressed,
Call back the times you were repressed;
Go back unto the turning point of life,
The sweet repressions of the future wife;
She, who was sweetheart of your youthful days,
Reproving kindly wayward ways.

THE SPELLING SCHOOL.

How cheery was the old-time spelling school
Given by the teacher in days of birch-rod rule.
Do you not still remember with what delight
We hailed the coming of that night?
The mud of winter, or the drizzling rain,
Caused us no anxiety or pain;
For we would bundle well and go
Be it through storm or winter's snow;
Do you not still remember the rosy cheeks
Which youth and health alone bespeaks?
His glasses were adjusted, with stick in hand,
He was determined all erect should stand;

Long lines were drawn up, like armies well arrayed
For field of action, not for dress parade;
And warm the contest, for there were those
Who faced each other like deadly foes!
And there were some who knew every word
In Webster's speller—for I have heard
It said, 'twas only by some grave mistake
That either side could honors take.
'Tis no fancied vision! Ah, I remember well
The merry times of the old-fashioned spell!
The night though dark, the sidewalk then unknown,
But other pleasures would these all atone;
For as we wandered home, her words so sweet,
I would not dare in after life repeat!
But you remember, though now you're silvered gray,
The words as well as 'twere but yesterday.
And you might tell, though this perhaps you'd hate—
The kiss was stolen—just at her father's gate!
These feats of skill by all were well enjoyed,
Think you not still, 'twas time quite well employed?
O, boyhood's happy days! We dream them o'er,
Forgetful now the ills we had in store,

As we go back unto our first old home,
To find none dearer 'neath earth's dome.
We see again with enrapt delight
The teachers in their power and might;
And learn obedience from their law
That ever guides our after life in awe.
Ah, yet those lessons first impressed in youth
Are full of thought — if not prosaic truth.
We find the boy a man, and watch his course,
And hail delightedly his manhood's force;
Then trace his truant youth, his wayward ways,
To find the man was made in birch-rod days.

THE DEBATE.

Can you call back the anguish of your look
When first you part in the discussion took?
His august presence, as he sat in state,
And eager watched your first debate!
Aye, Cushing's Manual, altho' 'twas new,
Produced not consternation then to you;
But stammering, speechless, with your heart in throat—

Forgetful the points you were quick to note;
The floor was sinking — it would soon give 'way —
You could not then on feet one thought convey.
Your effort was a failure — but his word
Was not reproof, and when from him you heard:
"The Halls of Congress would some day resound
With words from the speaker, intense, profound!"
You felt at once this life to you renewed,
As with new ideas you were imbued.
Confidence in yourself when once you've gained
Ever through life will be by you maintained.
And from that moment in forensic art
You eager were to take some active part;
Skilled in parliamentary law, you tried
With due deliberation to preside.
Your efforts then, if with success were crowned,
Speak but the man, in after life renowned.

Dear Hutson, my heart turns back to thee
As scenes of boyhood days come back to me —
Back to the river's bank I trace
My steps, with line, to the old fishing place.

We angle with the world in after years,
Trembling and cautious we battle it with fears,
While in our youth we cast a baited hook
With joyous glee into the babbling brook,
Watching contentedly until the bite
To land the bass and croppie with delight;
But busy man will scarce find time to know,
Or wander back to scenes of long ago,
Until old age creeps 'long with silent stealth
When first he realizes that in life his wealth
Is but contentment! Contented will I be
When the hour shall come, old Time is done with
    me—
When the clouds grow dark, and the eye grows dim,
And the Master's summon is to answer Him,
If they'll take me back to thee, old place so dear,
To rest 'side Him who gave my spirit here.

O, fleeting years! an unperceived decay
Beckons us ever onward day by day.
He will live best who lives the present seeing;
A wiser man, a happier being.

Expectant future is to us unknown;
Lives happy he who calls each day his own.
Tho' living present, we must ne'er forget
Our days of yore, dear unto memory yet.

THE EXHIBITION.

All is expectancy! The nervous strain
Is not much lessened by the six months' train.
Aye, from the boy of six, for one his age
"You'd scarce expect upon the stage."
Unto the lad much older grown,
Who realizes that the world's his own,
And thinks before few years have passed him by
To realize his expectations high.
Who thunders forth his eloquence in tones
Well calculated to melt the frigid zones;
Bidding defiance to all laws of speech
Save those the birch-rod master doth him teach.
O glorious youth, expectant hope!
Well calculated with the art of speech to cope.

The timid maiden with her voice so low,
How sweet her speech, "The Beauteous Snow."
And plays! Why, I remember to have seen
Them where they crowned the fairest maiden queen.
These recitations of our youthful days
I find more winning than the modern plays.
'Twas good McDonald, he that played the part
Of teacher in the terpsichorean art,
That furnished music with his band of ten;
Sweet players were they, all now cherished men.
Aye, well they swayed the audience — with delight
We recollect the music of that night.

Up rolls the curtain; bashfully steps forth
An humble youth; time tells his after worth;
And ever as the bell doth tap anew
Another comes — greets well the audience too.
"The Boy Stood on the Burning Deck "— while
    Mary
Told well her story of the Lambkin fairie;
While greater actors raised fine fierce disputes
And seemingly about "Bombastes' boots!"

The "Hardshell Sermon" and "Survive or Perish!"
"Webster's Reply to Hayne" I now cherish.
Ah, think you o'er in after life the part
You played that night in fine forensic art!
And wonder you that time will not efface
The memory of the birch-rod master's grace.

Then step we to that other grander stage,
The after years — riper, maturer age.
Look where we will, in life scan o'er and o'er,
You see the actors of the days of yore.
The lad who won, "The night we'd the spelling,"
Is sure to win in life. Where? No telling!
And he who tries, is eager to debate,
Rules certain after in affairs of state.
Life's exhibition and the school's the same;
The after years but tell of birch-rod fame.
Then turn we aside, one pitying glance
Tells that the after life is no romance
But real. Well is he who struggling tries
On earliest resources most relies.
The envious world, vast and battling throng,

Gives always way to him both well and strong.
The world is ever full, but learn to know
And dare its heights, look upward as you go.
The steeps of Fame though proudly you ascend,
It is through Toil that Fame her crown will lend.
Dare you the mysteries of skillful art,
Expect with work to take an active part;
Dare you gain success of any kind, be brave
Success demands mankind almost a slave.
No matter where, what part we take in life,
We may expect a constant struggling strife;
And only he who's best prepared, and strong,
Will mingle in life well, and mingle long.
Should fortune favor, frown not on the poor;
Go back, remember birch-rod days of yore.
In giddy forum should you meet success,
Remember strong the weak will oft oppress;
If born to rule, deal lightly with the mass;
Help, help the brother of the humble class.
These lessons all in former days were taught;
And must they perish — go for naught?
Would he permit the strong oppress the weak,

The high and mighty to deride the meek?
Were not his switches ofttimes used to pay
The tyrant youth who would oppress at play?
Heed then the lessons of thy youthful age,
In thy life's play upon the after stage;
And learn to know, no matter what thy ways,
Life's grandest lessons were in birch-rod days.

LITTLE LIGHTS.

In the sky little lights we frequently see,
Descending toward earth with a twinklesome glee;
Resplendent their course as through space they go dashing,
Soon to be out — 'tis the meteor's flashing.

They remind of the lives of little ones given
To us here on earth, from the kingdom of heaven;
They bud and they blossom awhile 'round our home,
Till the Heavenly Father bids them unto Him come.

The pangs of the parting will be ever the same;
And each sorrowing tear will burn as a flame,
To brighten the pathway of the little lives given,
In their journey from earth to the kingdom of heaven.

THE HARVEST OF DEATH.

Ah! harvest is ripe, and Death is around,
Securing his victims no matter where found,
And no greedier gatherer ever was known
Of the seeds of destruction, his agents have sown.
Not choice in his victims, not caring at all,
He sweeps down the line and gathers them all.
The young and the old, the rich and the poor,
Death gathers alike and brings to his door.
  He touches — all fall;
  They come at his call;
And he is but waiting to gather them all.

The sick and the weary, distressed and forlorn;
The gay and the merry, the proud'st e'er born;
The haughty and great, all lying in state,
He conquered by the same inevitable fate.
Nor wants he their lands, cares less for their gold:
Death is no miser, tho' grasping his hold;
And his eye seem'd to twinkle while he cast with a
  laugh

Their worldly possessions, like wind does the chaff.
>> He touches — they fall;
>> All come at his call;
And he is but waiting to gather them all.

Men striving and toiling from the time of their birth,
Depriving themselves of the luxuries of earth;
While neighbors, more lavish, build castles and revel
On the sins of this world, not unlike the devil.
Still others, ambitious for fame and renown,
Work body and mind till well broken down.
With hard striving statesman for temporal power,
Death touches each one ere the realizing hour.
>> He touches — they fall;
>> All come at his call;
And he is but waiting to gather them all.

And I sigh'd as I thought how Death gathers them in;
'Tis the penalty paid for man's primitive sin.
Then be cheerful and happy, altho' you be nigh,
Cross bravely Death's river when the time comes
>> to die;

For do not the merry, light-hearted and gay,
Make more out of life as they pass on their way?
Then do not have fear of an impending fate —
Postpone never happiness until 'tis too late.
    For all come at his call;
    When Death touches, we fall.
And he is but waiting to gather us all.

THE FELON'S SOLILOQUY.

Yes, I have killed him! And in bending low,
Rifling pockets, I saw his life's blood flow
Then stood aghast! For who can tell the sorrow
Even a life-long criminal will borrow
At sight of deed so cruel. Woe is me!
Outcast! Outlaw! Where'er on earth to flee!
Quick! Let me go! The very stillness of night
Makes doubly dread even a felon's flight!
And blood-leeches will soon be on my track,
Hounding, pursuing, soon to drag me back.
Where shall I fly? Is there no safety left
To one of law's protection now bereft?
Flee where I may, the lightning tracks my path
And justice scents my trail with pent-up wrath.
Hark! Ere the gray of morning's dawn, I fear
The sleuth-hounds will have trailed me and be near.
Surrender! Never! I will fast retreat
Back to the lonely swamps — for life is sweet.
"Throw up!" List! See! Now they surround me fast.
I yield — for in these times escape is past.
For even one, who hath law offended oft

Of God and man, and at man's nature scoffed!
But tracked and trailed, like a wild beast of prey,
I, felon, bend before the law's dread sway!
Oh, fate, thrice wretched! Henceforth in this cell
Remorse is mine, so bitter none can tell!
Behind the prison wall, a sin-cursed Cain,
Fettered in irons, bound in prison chain!
Aye, never more to breathe a breath that's free —
In sorrow waiting for the gallows tree!
Ah! We have felt the silent tear of time
Steal down the careworn, hardened face of crime.
Ah, crime! Foul crime! Thou hast indeed to grief
Brought all thy followers, and thy course is brief!
Methinks at times, thy seed is bred in man,
And curse the fate that brought us in thy van
To dire destruction! yet, we oft neglect
Best feelings of our conscience, and reflect
Not until the deed is done. Ill-fated born,
Flee from the path of sin, ere you, forlorn,
Fill some prison cell, or a felon's grave!
Fear laws of God and man and thyself save
Respect, as well as fear, for they alone
Bring peace on earth and happiness our own.

WHEN FORTUNE FROWNS.

The world's a cold sympathizer, when once dame
    fortune turns
Her smiling face and frowns upon us. Poverty
    then burns!
Cast then thyself upon its mercy, asking only bread,
If friendless and alone, a stone you'll be given
    instead.

Who cares for distress? There are few who care to
    trouble o'er
The needs of others. E'en waves will cast dis-
    mantled ship ashore.
The sorrow of an unfortunate one is but a drop
In the broad ocean of this earth, that causes few to
    stop.

Aye, busy, bustling humanity! Thou canst not stop
    to weep
With sorrowing ones. But each day thou seek'st
    to steep

Thyself in thine own pleasures, lusts, and pursuits
    for gain,
Too eagerly to sympathize with one another's pain.

Sorrowing, misguided, misdirected human kind!
    Ill-fated born!
Thou canst still retrieve adversity, still the world
    adorn!
Work! work! thou canst not find so sure a road to
    happiness —
Poverty will then banish, with its kindred care distress.

"My father worketh and I work"— graceful tribute
    given
To work, by Him who labored once on earth — now
    rules in Heaven.
Let then thy life's pleasure be thy life's work, for
    it will tell
In time's long race of years, if what thou doest,
    thou dost well.

KEATS.

A flower that blossomed only with the night!
   Rare and resplendent, 'twill in beauty glow,
   To dazzle and delight, and sweetness throw —
For out the darkness comes the glow of light.
Genius! Thou'rt a name ever to beam bright,
   And yet art coy and timid, till we know
   When one offends or proffers thee a blow,
Thou shrink'st involuntarily from the sight.
From this vale of darkness, with tale half told,
   Borne was Endymion! Blessed now above
With kindred spirits ever to repose!
High on the steep of fame his name enrolled,
   He sleeps Endymion's sleep! A Father's love —
An angel sent him from this world of woes.

THE MOCKING-BIRD.

A little gray bird flew in our oak tree,
Caroling sweetly, O brother, come — see!
I wonder his name! I'll list to his song!
I think I may tell as he warbles along!
      Jay, jay, jay,
      Ha, ha, hey!
Whoever heard, alth.' note is quite true —
      Jay, jay, jay;
Of a jay-bird in dress, and feathers not blue!

Gay, dashing fellow! How sprightly you sing;
Warbling the note of the blue-bird of Spring;
Aye! bounding aloft swift as an arrow —
Unless I mistake — 'tis the song of the sparrow;
      Whip-poor-will, whip-poor-will; —
      Oh, how shrill!
Cruel bird! I think you so silly —
      Whip-poor-will, whip-poor-will; —
Whoever knew of a bird whipping Willie?

Birdie, elated thy song I admire,
'Tis soft as the strains of the harp or the lyre,

I wonder — Ah! what a beautiful note
Is coming again from thy exquisite throat:
   Caw, caw, caw,
   La, la, la!
Indeed, little bird, do you not know —
   Caw, caw, caw ;—
You cannot deceive me to call you a crow.

Glorious song-bird, with voice like a lute;
Now piping away in tones of the flute;
O how I love thee! Birdie so free,
Exulting in thy song-mimicry;
   Mew, mew, mew,
   Ho, ho, you!
Never mind birdie, I will have none of that —
   Mew, mew, mew ;—
You think to delude me to call you a cat!

Like the red-bird you whistle; coo like the dove;
Of all the bird-songsters the daintiest love;
The shrill note of the hawk; chirp of the wren;
Imitate all the birds in our glen;

Bob White, Bob White,
Birdie, how bright!
You think, mimic bird, as other ways fail,
Bob White, Bob White;
To get little Miss to call you a quail.

My sweet, pretty bird, I'll no longer refrain,
Wonderful fellow! A name you disdain!
Mock-bird, I'll call thee! Ruler of Song!
Happiest bird 'mongst all the gay throng;
Kildeer, kildeer,
That note is queer!
Mocking-bird, talking-bird, with song melody —
Kildeer, kildeer;
Welcome, thrice welcome, our old oaken tree!

MY FLORIDA.

I would love to go where the sun shines bright,
When the wintry winds make cold the night;
When earth is chilled by a shivering blast
From the cheerless clouds, the skies o'ercast:

When the leaves are gone, and the trees look bare
With weeping branches from the sleet they wear;
When the ice has covered the streams and rills,
And grass lies hidden 'neath snow-clad hills.

Where the birds have flown I would love to go,
To a land of verdure where's no snow,
To a land of springtime, birds and flowers,
With babbling brooks and shady bowers.

Where the fig trees bear and the oranges blow;
Lemons ripen and bananas grow;
All nature's blooming and the birds are gay —
O, loveliest land — My Florida!

LINGERING AT THE GRAVE.

There are those who lonely linger 'round the silent,
    green-turfed grave
Of some dear beloved departed, whom the angels
    loving crave
For the spirit world above us, pure and spotless as
    the snow,
Where no sin can ever enter; where there is no pain
    or woe.
But the sorrowing tears they mingle with the life-
    less dust of earth,
And the silent prayers they utter, show us there is
    no dearth
Of deep, sad and bitter sorrow for the loved ones
    far away,
Gone to seek the bright to-morrow of our life's
    eternal day.

They are weeping for belov'd ones, and they feel
    the pain and sting
Of that last sad, tearful parting, which death's chill
    will ever bring;

Yet still there is one solace. 'Tis the promise that
    is given—
With them very soon they'll mingle in that kingdom
    we call Heaven.
And although they love to linger, and still wish
    them with us here,
And will sit and sigh, and sorrow at the grave, the
    pall, the bier —
They will smile with joy and gladness, for their
    spirit's only flown
To a purer realm of brightness — for God ever claims
    His own.

And they love to watch sweet flowers, and the
    daisies in the spring
Burst upon this world so brightly, 'round the lonely
    grave to cling;
And the shadows of the flowers as they fleeting pass
    away,
Tell the story of our being—earthly things must
    soon decay.
Yet the spirit ever lives, and seeks a world of joy
    and light,

And the Father ever kindly gives us his effulgence
    bright,
To show our earthly pathway, if we will follow in
    His lead.
Death is but a precious solace—if the living only
    heed.

Let them linger, linger, linger, till the last sad tear
    has flown
For the spirit-souls immortal, 'round our heavenly
    Father's throne;
Till the peeping stars of nightfall, in the distant
    heavens above,
Softly shed their glimmering beauty o'er the objects
    of their love.
Let them linger, linger, linger, till the aching heart-
    throbs cease,
And the weary mind shall slumber ever dreamily
    in peace;
It is not long until the hour when their spirit, too,
    shall rise,
There again to meet with loved ones in that home
    beyond the skies.

THE TRAIN.

Hear the train!
It comes again.
Travelers, hurrying to and fro,
Wait impatiently to go
On their journey, near or far,
Snugly housed in palace car.
Mile-posts past them quickly blend,
Swift they reach their destined end.
The homeward journey's safely made,
The business man to place of trade.
  Flying train,
  Speed on thy way again!

Hear the train!
Thundering on again.
Wonderful its rapid gait,
Moving millions' worth of freight,
Bearing on the golden grain,
Reaped on fertile western plain;

Carrying trade from distant shore,
Earth's productions to our door;
Speed them on; all nations bind,
Showering blessings on mankind.
  Useful train,
   Speed on again!

  Hear the train
  Dash on again!
Begrimed with coal the fireman stands;
Grasping the reins with strong firm hands.
The engineer, thro' rain and sleet,
Bravely drives his engine neat.
Ah! in thy care, brave knights of train,
The lives of countless souls remain.
Noble thy task and fearless done,
True hearts, no braver 'neath the sun.
  Speed, gallant train,
   Through storm and rain.

Flashing train,
Speed on again!
Greatest blessing giv'n to man,
Civilization in thy van.
Ah! thy wheels we gladly hail,
Carrying merchandize and mail.
Miles are multiplied each hour,
Thro' thy wonder-working power;
And distance — once a king so great,
Like time, thou now dost subjugate.
Glorious train,
Speed on again!

THE TREE AND THE ROSE.

One day boasting,
    An Oak-Tree said
Unto a Brier-Rose,
    With low-bent head:

"Barns and bridges
    Are built of me;
Towns and cities —
    I'm a useful tree.

"You a Brier-Rose,
    Are of little use —
To the busy world
    A mere excuse!"

"Sir," said Brier-Rose,
    "Happy the hours,
Seeing Fair-One
    Gather my flowers.

"Wreathes of roses,
 Buds on the stem,
Lovely garlands
 I give to them."

The giant tree —
 The boasting Oak,
Soon lay fell'd
 By woodman's stroke.

But the little Rose
 Still grows each year,—
Her fragrant flowers
 To the world so dear.

So, isn't it best
 Quite oft to be
A Brier-Rose
 Than a boasting-tree?

THE CROSS, ILL-NATURED MAN.

Roam, roam the wide world over,
    Search every corner well;
Go, go, my winsome rover,
    Search every nook and dell;
And then come back and tell me,
    In all thy wanderings 'round,
Of all the vermin, reptile,
    Can any one be found
That can compare for meanness
    With a cross, ill-natured man?
The rover smiled in meekness:
    No place where one can scan,
In all my wanderings 'round,
    Can such a one be found.

The spider stings with poison;
    The scorpion unto death;
The flea doth tickle o'er our leg;
    The ghost doth take our breath.

But, Oh! you cross, ill-natured man;
 You snarling, snapping creature;
You are the leader of the van,
 The meanest of all torture.
You poise our finer feelings;
 You pierce us like a dart;
The day so warm and sunny —
 You make it cold and dark:
Should anyone seem funny
 It breaks your jealous heart.

The pretty, prattling children,
 Into a corner shy;
Of chilling words, so 'fraid are they,
 Whenever thou art by.
Your home is made so wretched
 That all do dread thy gaze;
In everything thou art finding fault
 In many hundred ways.
Thy favorite dog thou scoldest;
 Thy wife and children too,

And when they plead for mercy
    Thou scarest them from thy view;
And all are glad, when you are gone,
    To rid themselves of you.

Ah! well thou said'st, my rover,
    In all thy wanderings 'round,
In searching this world over
    No one thing could be found
That can give to us such torture,
    That can give to us such pain,
As — as this living creature —
    A cross, ill-natured man.
Now, should any of our readers
    Be ill-naturedly inclined,
I trust they will immediately
    Do penance till they find
The greatest blessing of this earth —
    Is a sweet contented mind.

THE ORATOR.

Sweet silver tongue! 'Tis with delight
We listen to thy power and might
In tones deep, ringing, soft and clear;
When voicing justice and the right
Thou'lt never fail man's heart to near.

Aye, magic voice! Refined, polite —
Deeds bold and daring thou canst incite:
Or bring the eye at will to tear —
    Sweet silver tongue.

Art consummate! Thy lofty flight,
Will unto thee at all times plight
All lovers of pure speech who hear:—
True eloquence at dazzling height
Is ever to mankind most dear —
    Sweet silver tongue.

SIC ITER AD ASTRA.

Would you attain to greatness,
   In any living sphere,
And leave a never-dying name,
   You must always persevere.
Let not the clouds of darkness
   Enshroud you in their gloom,
But battle bravely onward,
   Battle to the tomb.
Ah! he who wins must labor,
   And this his watchword be:
Work, labor, without ceasing,
   Sic iter ad astra.

When sorrows hover o'er you,
   And life seems dark and drear,
Press onward, these regardless,
   And always take good cheer:
For no end was e'er accomplished
   By the desponding one.

Remember, all's not darkness,
   The night gives way to morn;
For let the day be as it may,
   Our harvest time is always gay.
Press onward — never ceasing,
   Sic iter ad astra.

Would you a warrior be,
   With never-dying fame;
For thy heroic greatness
   Leave an everlasting name:
You must go and battle bravely,
   Have never, never fear,
And when the danger's greatest
   Bring all thy powers to bear.
The battle may rage fiercely,
   The victory sure, if we
Press onward without ceasing,
   Sic iter ad astra.

Yes, in the hour of conflict,
    When danger threatens most,
And Death's dread missiles 'round you fall,
    Be firm — still at thy post,
For 'tis never the faint-hearted
    Who win in any strife ;
But with will and courage true
    You will win throughout this life.
Then let thy motto always be,
    Forever, ever say:
On, on till victory,
    Sic iter ad astra.

WHAT IS FAME?

And what is Fame?
A dazzling name,
Like a meteoric star;
A moment on
And then 'tis gone,
Away, away so far.

Aye, who can tell,
What work, and well,
Will bring it in our grasp?
Like melting snow,
'Tis quick to go,
Ere mortals can it clasp.

Man's never still,
But ever will —
Ambition his desire —
Seek for a name;
To court proud Fame,
Alone he will aspire.

Still, life's made bright,
Like new-born light,
That doth each morning shine;
And toiling man
Will plan and plan
In search for Fame divine!

LOVE'S ARROWS.

Treacherous thy arrows, Love,
    Poisonous thy darts;
We place them in our quivers, Love,
    Forgetting broken hearts;
You bid us be in welcome, Love,
    We blindly, madly sing;
Hope's sweetest smile is with us, Love,
    Till thou thy arrows fling.

You play, you fondle, with your prize,
    Led captive by thy love;
You tease, torment us, with thine eyes —
    Sweet starlights like above!
We thy caresses glad embrace,
    Not fearful of thy sting;
We yield to beauty and thy grace,
    Till thou thy arrows fling.

Yet seek we for thy arrows, Love,
  And gather, o'er and o'er,
Thy smarting, stinging, piercing darts,
  Forgetting those of yore.
What would life be without them, Love?
  We'll to them always cling;
Trust to thy graciousness, O Love,
  Till thou thy arrows fling.

IN FANCY DREAMING.

You may muse in fancy dreaming,
   But the Real will appear;
Bright the rainbow-colors seeming,
   Yet the clouds are always near.

But altho' the storm-clouds gather,
   They will quickly pass away:
And the gloomiest of life's weather
   Brings the most effulgent day.

And 'tis folly to be losing
   Time that's given us by our God;
But be tireless, faithful using
   Till we lie beneath the sod.

'Tis a debt that you are owing
   To the Giver of your life,
To be up and ever doing —
   Ceaseless is the appointed strife!

Quit thy dreams! and go with feeling,
   Go with joy into the sea
Of life's duties, ever dealing
   With a heart both light and free!

OLD AGE.

Old Age, we thee abhor!
Stay off! For we deplore
The time which will us bring
Unto thee an offering!

Thy scythe! An emblem bright!
Plainly we see as night
Of age creeps unawares,
Till thy grim visage stares!

Aye, still how true, and yet
How many will forget
Each moment, hour and day,
Presses us on thy way!

Rudderless, like ship tost
On Time's waves, all are lost;
Death will our pathways sweep
Mortal—we only weep!

Silvered by years, we bend,
Infirm, at thy decree;
Reach at our journey's end—
Unknown eternity.

TO MY WIFE.

ON OUR TWENTY-FIRST ANNIVERSARY.

Swiftly the years go by,
   'Tis one and twenty now
Since you, my wife, and I,
   Took each a lasting vow:
Through life to journey without fear
And be unto each other dear.

Our spring of life is o'er;
   Our summer's sun, once bright,
Shines on us now no more;
   But autumn brings delight:
For we can reap the harvest's yield
And garner from a fruitful field.

Life's winter soon we'll near,
   But we will happy be;
For I shall have no fear,
   Since thou wilt be with me:
And in the time of my decline
My comfort is thou wilt be mine.

The sun effulgent gleams
    At dawning of the day;
But more in beauty beams
    As evening fades away:
And in the evening of our life
Thou'lt be to me the dearest wife.

OUR COUNTRY HOME.

Fondly I prize my country home,
    And ever loved it dearly;
No other place, where'er I roam,
    Time passes half so cheerly;
The morning birds break forth in song
    And sing to me so early,
With roses blooming summer long,
    Fed by the dew so pearly.

The lilacs blossom by the gate,
    Birds twitter in their bowers;
While golden maples, old and great,
    Brush their purple-tinted flowers;
Old's the orchard, with fruit and vine;
    And the oak trees on our lawn,
With swing, where happy children, mine,
    Make glad the morning's dawn.

Here fragrant blooms the old pear tree;
    Pure white's the plumwood's blossom;

Home ladened wings the honey-bee,
    Her treasures from earth's bosom.
The mocking-bird with joyful notes,
    Gladdening the woodland's ring,
With mimic song of warbling throats,
    Sweet harbingers of the spring.

Happily here I spend my days,
    With wife and children dearie,
Life's sunshine doth dispel the haze,
    And we're content and merry.
'Tis ever dear unto the heart,
    Its pleasures are not glary;
Yet health and strength it doth impart,
    Its joys we would not vary.

BETTER THAN GOLD.

Blessed children with hearts bold,
What is better far than gold?
Health and strength, two things grand,
Coming from His loving hand,
Are of value more ten fold —
Better, better far than gold.

Faith in God, and Charity,
Are two branches of a tree,
Of a Wisdom Tree from Heaven,
Tree of Knowledge from God given!
Keep its teachings as you're told —
You'll be richer far than gold.

Learn a little from this life,
Man is mortal, 'tis a strife;
And that strife should ever be
Few are chosen, select are ye!
Work for God, with courage bold,
'Twill be better far than gold.

Earthly riches, worldly wealth,
Which may leave us as by stealth;
Grandeur, glory, pomp of power;
Fancied visions of the hour,
Are in life a fleeting show,
And quite valueless we know.

IDLE-WHILES.

See the idle moments fly,
Who can save them, you and I?
We can use them, too, with grace,
We can mould them into place;
   Change them into sunny smiles —
   Idle moments — idle-whiles!

Hear the moments as they fly!
Catch them! as they pass you by:
You can make them serve you well,
Better far than I can tell!
   Never let one you beguile —
   Idle moment — idle-while!

Feel the moments as they go,
Quickly passing — never slow!
They can make you happy hours
By their wonder-working powers!
   Can you lose and reconcile
   Idle moment — idle-while?

Whiling moments as they flee;
Whiling time agreeably;
Whiling time in reverie!
Who will ever us revile,
  May I ask you, with a smile,
  Should we lose one after while?

THE TWILIGHT SHADES.

The twilight shades of night appear,
   As I sit silent, lonely here,
Watching the rifting clouds on high
   Swiftly passing each other by.
The fitful stars shine out so bright,
   As nature dons her robes of night;
'Tis time for weary eyes to close
   In sleep — kind Nature's sweet repose.

The low, sad chirp of insect wail,
   Alone doth cheerless hours regale,
Save ripplings from yon babbling brook,
   That greet me in this quiet nook.
All Nature's still! The weary borne
   To peaceful rest from cares till morn;
And hushed in the stillness of the night
   Are all the busy sounds of light.

I fancied in yon peeping star
   A home for beings, tho' afar,
Who now are free from sin and vice
   And dwell with God in paradise.

I saw in vision's viewless space,
  Spirit forms of a blissful race,
Who trod of yore the unseen way
  That leads to life's eternal day.

Eternity! O endless years!
  Shall mortal fear thee! Banish fears!
Put trust in Him who gave to thee
  A soul to save for eternity.
Along time rolls! It waits for none!
  It claims alike the old, the young;
Earth's but a season to begin
  To save the soul once lost in sin.

And as I dreamed, 'way sped the night,
  With flickering moon and starry light:
Emblem of death! when 'neath the sod
  We wait the coming of our God.
So, as the night gives way to morn,
  We'll to undying life be born;
The dawn of lovely morning bright
  Is emblem of the world of light.

THE BATTLE-FLAG.

Battle-flag, glittering in sunlight and gold,
On each starry crest of thy swelling fold
The name of an hundred battles told.
Recall the glories, O comrade, when
It wav'd on the field o'er a thousand men,
While we marched to the field of battle;
    then
This flag of ours was new,
With its silvery stars, on a field of blue,
And bright, broad stripes commingling,
    too.

Omen of victory! to us unfold
Scenes of thy carnage as yet untold —
Deeds of thy warfare, brave and bold.
Read and rehearse with blinding tears
The valor and courage of volunteers —
Gather the trophies for coming years —
Who gave their lives in the cause of right
And march'd to the front in gallant fight,
Led by our flag of red, blue and white.

Hail! noble flag, with thy battle scars!
Glorious blending of immortal stars!
Grand old souvenir of our wars!
Oft hast thou gladden'd the soldier's life
On struggling fields when battles rife,
Rainbowing the clouds of deadly strife.
And now that the storm of war has fled,
Bespangl'd banner of blue, white and red,
May thy mem'ry ever bright luster shed.

THE TEMPLAR.

Gaily bedight, the gallant Knight
    Comes charging o'er the mead ;
His shining lance doth me entrance,
    As well his dashing steed.
O Knight of old, on charger bold,
    Thou'lt never suffer loss,
All know thy fame, and prize thy name,
    You wear the Sacred Cross !

In the cause of Right thou wast a Knight—
    Child of humility —
And battled brave, God's land to save,
    With great ability.
Fervent thy zeal, for Christian weal
    Thou hast been battling long ;
And holy sod, by the will of God,
    You've rescued from the wrong!

Take up thy shield, and thy sword wield
    In honor of the just ;
Religion's view, the Christian's too,
    Is now thy sacred trust;

The orphan's name, the maiden's fame,
    The lonely widow's part,
To thy defense, thence bravely hence,
    Go! Valorous thou art!

O brothers all, come at his call;—
    Around the sacred throne,
Let us invite each gallant Knight,
    To sacrifice his own;
For the Lord above, who will us love,
    As we fall in His line;
The Great we praise, will all us raise—
    We conquer in this Sign!

Gaily bedight, O gallant Knight,
    Charging o'er the mead;
Thy shining lance doth still entrance,
    As well thy dashing steed!
And Knight of old, on charger bold,
    Thou'lt never suffer loss,
The God above will ever love,
    Who wears His Sacred Cross!

FRIENDSHIP'S DISEASE.

A disease to friendship quite fatal,
   No matter how strong the tie be,
Is little dislikes; gradual decay;
   Slight causes very trifling to see.

The angry in time we may reconcile;
   The injured we can compensate:
Those who refuse all desire to be pleased,
   Friendship will never rejuvenate.

Like frosts of the Autumn that wither the
      rose,
   Scatter its leaves, the branches make
      bare;
The chill of distrust which silently grows,
   Friendships of life will ever impair.

MOCKING-BIRD AND JAY.

One summer's day
A saucy jay
Said to a mocking-bird:
"In handsome blue,
I'm gayer than you,
Greatly to be preferred!

"I've a royal crest,
And fine blue vest,
Feathers of richest hue!
I daily spat,
And social chat,
Gaily with neighbors too!"

Your royal crest,
And fine blue vest,
Feathers of richest hue!
Are very fine,
Much more than mine,
I grant that all to you!

"But, coxcomb bold,
Loquacious scold —
Given to aspersion!
There's scarce a bird,
'Mong all I've heard,
Hath not for thee aversion.

"Aye, bird so gay,
Let me this say,
Known I am by my song;
Where'er I fly
Welcome am I —
Not so your finical throng."

REJECTED.

There is no word that one can find
That gives more anguish to the mind,
    Though each word be inspected,
As this one, cruelest of its kind —
        Rejected.

To man who earns his daily bread,
Each day doth labor without dread,—
    Life's hardships hath suspected;
Could more remorseless word be said —
        Rejected!

For are not all men here below,
Entitled to some little show
    In life to be protected?
How cruel then must be the blow —
        Rejected!

Inhuman word! Where'er thou art,
You wound the aching, sobbing heart,
    Who with life's cares dejected
Doth sorrow underneath thy smart—
        Rejected!

FAIL NOT.

Fail not, my Child, whose pathway's sown
   With fortune's smiles and flowers,
To help the poor less-favored one
   Beguile the weary hours.

And fail not, Man, throughout this life,
   To do what good you can;
The struggle's long, and fierce the strife,
   Help then thy fellow-man !

Mother, fail not thy child to raise,
   Who will this world control,
To sing of Him in songs of praise—
   The giver of his soul.

Father, thy son fail not to teach
   When first young life buds forth;
Life's highest stations he may reach,
   Success the effort's worth.

Ah, some may search but fail to find
   The ladder-rounds of fame ;
But none need fail to leave behind
   A pure and spotless name.

CUPID AND DEATH.

Cupid, the God of Youth and Love,
  Weary of play and faint with heat,
Wandering down into Death's Grove,
  Into his grotto beat retreat.

Beautiful darts as ever graced,
  Sent from the angel world above,
Cupid had in his quiver placed —
  Piercing arrows of Youth, and Love.

Down on the floor, in careless haste,
  Cupid thought there to rest him well;
The lovely arrows therein placed
  Soon from their shining quiver fell;

And scattered o'er his cave, pell-mell,
  Death had arrows of exquisite make:
Cupid, waking, could never tell
  His own from Death's, or which to take.

Death's darts with Love, and Love's with
       Death,
  Were now mingled in luckless ruth;

Tho' sweet sometimes, the poisonous breath
   Of old grim Death isn't good for Youth!

And since that day Love has been blind
   Seemingly, to every fate;
And Love is now to Death resigned,
   Often choosing him for a mate.

And Death has kissed Love's young and old,
   No matter how timid or shy:
Death since with Youth is very bold,
   And never passes Love by.

THE FELON'S DREAM.

Slumbering I lay in prison cot,
   In peaceful dreams, all woes forgot.
Repose! How sweet! 'Twas scarcely
      marred
   By heavy tramp of prison guard.

Back to my home in dreams I went;
   Back to that place I childhood spent;
Mingling there in merriest glee
   Again with those quite dear to me.

I clasped in fond embrace once more
   A mother's form! Heard her implore
In bitter anguish, God to spare
   A truant son — an only care!

Friendly faces were gathered around,
   Welcoming home a lost one found;
I had resolved to quit my sin —
   I felt a change of heart within!

It was a dream — and when I 'woke
   The walls of prison on me broke;
I felt to dry a felon's face
   Saddest, dreariest of his race!

I said: "This cruel fate seems hard!"
   'Twas only mocked by tramp of guard.
Cruel's the pang! Deep is the sting!
   A lonely cell to felons bring!

Deal not harshly! Speak not ill!
   Fate was 'gainst him —'gainst him still;
Who sleeps behind this prison wall:—
   There's none so strong but what may fall.

SWEET LADY, I LOVE THY FAIR FACE.

Sweet lady, I love thy fair face,
   And wish, oh wish, that it were mine;
For beauty, form, and lovely grace
   Is now, and ever will be thine!

The night with lowering clouds and dark
   Has beauteous flashings in the sky;
But e'en the brilliant lightning's spark
   Will not match the luster of thine eye!

And yet, sweet lady, kind and true,
   Why I adore thy face,
I seek the rose in morning's dew,
   Alone pure innocence to trace.

God has implanted in our breast
   A love for all that's pure;
Life's pleasures man may go in quest —
   Alone doth woman lure.

THE SUNNY SOUTHERN HOME.

    I ever love to see
    The sweet magnolia tree.
Dance its leaves in the breezes of the morn;
    Where the sun will ever glow,
    And gentle zephyrs blow
O'er the fields of cotton and the corn.

    'Tis nature's sweet retreat,
    Where lovers gladsome meet;
Daisies in the springtime there first come;
    And the ever-blooming rose
    Is free from wintry snows,
In the dear old sunny southern home.

    You wander where you will,
    Its memory ever still
Will cling to your heart as you roam;
    For birds are ever gay
    In sweetly singing lay,
In the dear old sunny southern home.

And the true hearts we there find
Will ever us remind,
There is on earth no other dome,
So dear to every heart,
Compelled from there to part,
As the dear old sunny southern home.

MINE, ONLY MINE.

Wilt thou not be my dearest,
    As we journey down life's stream;
And be to me the nearest,
    My fondest hope and dream?
Oh, tell me that you love me,
    And be forever mine;
By the Heavens above thee,
    I pledge my heart to thine!

By the evening shadows,
    When the sun sinks in the west;
By the bloom of meadows,
    I will vow to love thee best!
Ever will I adore thee,
    True love it is divine;
Oh, list while I implore thee,
    Be mine, only mine!

Let others love the morning,
    With the sun and beauty's light;

The smile now thee adorning
   Is to me a sweeter sight.
Oh, love is like a flower —
   Plucked from the stem, it dies,
While in its sylvan bower
   On earth naught more we prize.

AUTUMN LEAVES.

See the Autumn leaves go flying,
    Flying with the swift-winged breeze;
And the winter winds are sighing,
    Sighing to the leafless trees!

Hear them as they gently rustle;
    Watch them chase each other 'round:
They are ever in a bustle
    Dancing o'er the green-turfed ground.

See them in the air go sailing,
    As the whirlwind sucks them on:
Hear them rattle, like 't were hailing,
    Rattle, rattle on the lawn!

Helpless are the little leaflets;
    To be carried soon away
Far adown the swirling streamlets;
    There to perish and decay.

True in life all things must perish;
    Ever bright the morning's dawn;
Still, life's fondest hopes we cherish
    Decay like leaves upon the lawn.

MADIE GREEN.

In the twilight of an evening,
   In the dear old month of June,
When the air was filled with fragrance —
   When the roses were in bloom;
I met by chance a maiden,
   Fair, fair as ever was seen,
And I loved her from that moment —
   Pretty, pretty Madie Green.
      Never was a lovelier lady,
         None fairer have I seen
      Than my little dark-eyed Madie —
         Pretty, pretty Madie Green.

True, there is in life's oasis,
   One sweet solace given man —
'Tis a pure and spotless woman,
   She who all our sorrows can
Make light as gentle zephyrs
   As they whisper to the trees,
When the leaflets softly rustle,
   Fanned by the summer's gentle breeze.

Never was a lovelier lady,
    None fairer have I seen
Than my little dark-eyed Madie —
    Pretty, pretty Madie Green.

The rose, our fairest flower,
    Where the bee will ever come,
Gathering sweetness every hour,
    To bear unto its home —
Will not equal pretty Madie,
    Tho' it be of loveliest hue,
And we gather flower and leaflet
    Bathed in morning's early dew.
    Never was a lovelier lady,
        None fairer have I seen
    Than my little dark-eyed Madie —
        Pretty, pretty Madie Green.

While now I sit in silence,
    O'er other days I con,
I remember still, with sadness,
    That summer's day now gone;

I remember her dark tresses;
　Her bright and lustrous eyes;
But her loving, dear caresses,
　Most of all I highly prize.
　　Never was a lovelier lady,
　　　None fairer have I seen,
　　Than my little dark-eyed Madie —
　　Pretty, pretty Madie Green.

Still the clouds will gather o'er me,
　As I murmur this my song;
And I pray thee, Lord, restore me
　To the girl I've loved so long;
And when this life is ended,
　And I'm borne away to rest,
May my spirit there be blended
　With the one I loved the best.
　　Never was a lovelier lady,
　　　None fairer have I seen,
　　Than my little dark-eyed Madie —
　　Pretty, pretty Madie Green.

SLEEP AND HOPE.

When the world is dark, and all is drear,
And there is naught to cheer us here;
When friends prove false, and fickle, too,
And the things we love are dimmed to view;
Sweet comforter, let my weary head
Be couched upon thy pillowy bed;
Then waft me in ethereal dreams,
And take me 'way from earthly themes;
While angel-images hover 'round,
O peace, be mine, in sleep so sound!

Take, take me from this world afar,
And thou sweet Sleep, as guiding-star,
Wilt thou not find some place above,
Where all is hope, where all is love?
Where all is gladness, all is joy,
And cares of life no more annoy?
Where man to brother can be just?
Where all are honest — all can trust?
Where cheat and strife can harm no more;
And war's dread conflicts all are o'er?

Where fear our vision ne'er can fright,
And is dispelled, like day doth night;
All life's imagined ills are gone,
Unlike the sun, no more to dawn!
Where malice with resentless eye,
Thirsts not to make more misery;
And misanthropy is not found,
To mar our joys the season 'round,
Making us miserable without hope,
As vainly on with life we cope?

Where is no sadness, that doth rend
The heart full sore with tears, and blend
It with despondency and despair,
To make earth's beings wretched as they
    are?
Where jealousy, which we oft endure,
That rather would the sun obscure,
Than see another enjoy its light —
Emulous of all who seek the right —
Is gone forever — sin-cursed mien,
Whenever hated, wherever seen?

Where scorn and envy both must toil —
Green monsters of earth's sinful soil —
Till their necks goad blue with disdain?
Another's pleasure is to them pain.
Where pride, disdainful, cold and chill,
Becomes subservient to our will;
And contempt, bitter, which doth deride,
Is humbled like its neighbor, pride?
Where, changed to mercy, all may feel
The bitter pangs they used to deal?

A heavenly thing, O Sleep, to dream,
And let the troubled spirit gleam
And beam in brightness! Shine afar —
Since Hope is now our guiding-star!
Pandora, careless of man's want,
Let from her jar life's ills, to haunt
Our visions, pleasures, passions, joys,
With fears, adversities, griefs, annoys,
That follow, as through life we grope —
The lid was closed alone on Hope!

THE TRAITOR BIRD.

"Let me go, good Master Falconer,"
   A little Quail once said;
Who being caught within a net,
   Thought thus to save its head.

"I will decoy some other quails,
   At least a dozen more,
And get them safely in your net,
   If you will ope' your door."

"No," cried the man, "I'll not let out,
   Whate'er I might have done,
The treacherous bird within my net;
   The traitor shall not run!

There is no death too hard for him
   Who will a friend betray;
And I'll not spare you, traitor bird,
   To live another day!"

THE WORLD IS COLD, SO DREARY.

The world is cold, so dreary,
   Few warm hearts do we find;
Life's path to me is weary,
   And troubled is my mind.
Oh, I'm so sad to-day, Mary,
   Clouds hover o'er and o'er;
I think alone of thee, Mary,
   Alone thee I adore.

I wish sometimes myself, Mary,
   In the cold, damp grave, at rest;
Where sleeps the dead in peace, Mary,
   Calm and Heavenly blest.
Where no taunts and jeers are heard, Mary,
   Where no foe can ever blame;
Where rich and poor are clothed, Mary,
   In nature's garb the same.

I sometimes think and fear, Mary,
   There's no better world than this;

That man who is sin-cursed, Mary,
    Can e'er hope to reach bliss!
But we know the Savior's promised
    If we hearken to his call,
He will bid us welcome, enter,—
    There's room above for all.

THE WABASH.

Beautiful river by Hutson,
   With thy silvery sheet of blue;
Ever sluggishly moving onward
   Like a panoramic view.

While now I trace thy meandering course
   From the old Town down to the bend,
A feeling of sadness comes o'er me
   As the journey onward I wend:

To think of the scenes of my childhood,
   Of the ones who used to stray
Along with me down the river's banks,
   Where now I stroll to-day·

To watch for the landmarks of boyhood,
   And find that the river's surge
Swept them away—like the friends of
      youth,
   The winds sigh only the dirge.

Once gaily adown thee, old river,
   In his birchen bark canoe,
Floated the Indian warrior,
   With his maiden of dusky hue.

Upon thy banks were his councils,
   Around brightly glowing fires;
The mossy mounds near the river's brink —
   The graves of ancestral sires.

The warrior has gone from thy forests,
   And his race is almost run;
Driven by the white men westward
   With the course of the setting sun.

But thy grand old oaks and thy elms,
   That were once his shelter and pride,
Still nod to the rippling waters
   As they grow by the river's side.

Flow on, O beautiful river!
   Flow gently on to the sea;
I'll watch thy waters a little while —
   Then the Master will summon me.

WHO MAY SERVE WELL.

A lion was intent on sleep,
When o'er his limbs a Mouse would creep;
Angered, he caught it with a sweep,
    And chiding, said ;
"'Tis useless, Mouse, in tears to weep,
    I'll strike you dead!"

Piteously, with tearful eye,
The mouse then made this sad reply:
"Oh, master! Do not let me die!
    I can repay
The life you spare, even I,
    The act some day!"

Despicably small he thought him; so,
Laughing, the lion let him go;
Saying, "Mouse, I'll spare you, though
    If with my paw
I'd strike you just a little blow,
    I'd crush your jaw!"

Shortly after, it chanced one day,
The lion was pursuing prey.
Some hunters who had come that way
    Set nets they brought.
The lion, bounding lithe and gay,
    Was in them caught.

The lion, fast, set up a roar.
Hearing, the mouse ran nimbly o'er,
And meshes binding limbs, now sore,
    Began to gnaw;
From off the lion quickly tore
    With little jaw.

Thankful, the lion, now more wise,
Said, "Little things we oft despise,
In after life we highly prize;
    For none can tell,
Simply in judging by the size,
    Who may serve well!"

DRONES vs. BEES.

Once in a *Nisi Prius* court,
   Judge Wasp called up a case,
A suit about some honey-comb,
   Among the insect race.

The action was replevin,
   Some drones sued out the writ,
Claiming both honey and the comb,
   Which the bees could not admit;

But pleaded property in themselves,
   And property in their queen;
Non cepit, non detinuit, too,
   On property had a lien.

Each party then a jury waived,
   The issues being closed;
To try the case before the judge,
   Both parties then proposed.

Judge Wasp then said: "You are alike,
   In color, shape and size;
I'll test the case by evidence,
   In manner seeming wise.

I'll give unto you each a hive,
  To make new comb and cell;
When filled, the honey I will taste —
  Go quick and do it well!"

The bees assented to the plan,
  And comb began to make:
The drones kept idle, to a man,
  To work they would not take.

"'Tis plain to see, unto the bee
  The honey does belong,
I'll adjudge the case, upon its face,
  Unto the working throng.

" For he who can not make the comb,
  The honey should not claim;
On every issue, bees have won;"
  Judge Wasp then gave them same.

'Tis thus the idle always lose,
  They're worthless, to a man;
If to succeed in life you choose,
  To work's the only plan.

DAME FORTUNE.

O'ercome with fatigue from journey long,
    A young man, weary and tired, fell
Quite fast asleep, on the very brink
    Of a deep and dangerous well.
Dame Fortune, seeing the danger, said:
    "Wake up, wake up, wake up, my man!"
And rousing him from his slumber, then
    Said, chiding, "Sir, all of your clan,
Blame me quite often for troubles, when
    The folly is simply with you men!"

"You see, the censure is thrown upon me
    By all of the human kind;
When in truth, I know and always see
    The most of them go it blind!
Great calamities which them befall,
    Is folly they bring of their own;
Imputable to me? Not at all,
    I wish I could make it known—
All more or less masters are of fate,
    Must think for themselves, not on me
        wait!"

Dame Fortune then went tripping away,
  Singing sweetly this merry song:
"Men mortal, I cannot with you stay,
  Yet I'll frequently join your throng:
Tho' I'm fickle as fickle can be,
  Try me ever to court and wed,
By the use of sense and industry,
  My favors around you I'll shed:
For those who court fortune, well should
      know
  The idle and vicious have no show."

AVARICE.

The world is full of men who try in vain,
Without much effort riches to obtain;
Who risk in folly the little they possess,
And bring themselves to penury and distress.
Never content with what the Lord doth give,
They'd rather starve, than not in affluence live.

Avarice will get us into trouble,
When we're too anxious wealth to double;
Into wealth's door we sometimes gain ingress
To find we've lost the little we possess:
Becoming greedy beyond all measure,
We lose our all seeking more treasure.

A certain man, I read in fable old,
Possessed a goose, that laid an egg of gold
Each day—an income stated, all his days—
The best of incomes—one that certain pays;
But dissatisfied with this fortune slow,
He killed the goose, her treasures all to know.

Within he thought a wealth of gold to see.
But found her the same as any goose would be;
The man so miserly was quick to rue it,
Forsooth he lost a fortune through it.
Risk not thy all, lest it may go by stealth
In vainly trying to amass great wealth.

THE THRUSH.

Sweet messenger of morning, I love well
   Thy piping notes of fitful, fervent glee!
   Swinging aloft on topmost limb of tree;
Soft as flute tones thy bird-song on me fell;
Then like the tinkling of a distant bell
   Thy sweet notes die, and echoes come to me,
Soothing the morning dreams delightfully,
As rose the sun the dawn of day to tell.
   Sing, warbler, sing! To stay is thy delight
   In shaded dells where runs the babbling brook,
O'erhung with alder bush; where 'tis thy right
To hide thy nest in wild-vined laurel nook;
   Each lovely morn of spring, O bird so bright,
   I will for thee listen: for thee I'll look.

UNION IS STRENGTH.

A family of sons a father had
Who perpetually treated each other bad;
And no exhortations would take from their sire,
But constantly gave some vent to their ire.
Determined to illustrate the ills of dissension,
To a bundle of sticks he called their attention,
Then, giving the bundle to each in succession —
"Break it!" he cried. They made no impression.
Then out of the bundle, each a single stick took.
"Break it!" he cried. The stick easily broke.
Then he addressed them: "My sons, if you are
United in mind, and never at war,
Like a bundle of sticks, well bound together,
Success of the one means success of the other."

IDLY-HEEDING.

"Leave off crying, this instant, or I'll throw
You out at the window, to the Wolf below!"
"What! I recognize the voice of the nurse—
As I am hungry I might fare worse;
What would be more excellent than a fine fat child,"
And the greedy Wolf looked up and smiled:

Thinking the nurse as good as her word,
To wait for the child, the Wolf preferred;
For the hungry Wolf had searched all that day
In vain for food till he came that way:
And he waited there till the day was done,
And darkness came with the setting sun.

As the twilight shades stole into the house,
The lovely child was still as a mouse;
Save singing its lullaby sweet as a lark —
Going to sleep with the evening dark:
Fondling her child the nurse said in a low breath:
"If the Wolf comes now, I'll beat him to death!"

But the words were caught on the dewy air
By the Wolf, who heard them with despair;
Disappointed and hungry he turned to go,
Muttering these words in accents low:
" This comes by heeding those who ofttimes say
Things they never intend, day after day!"

OUR FAITHFUL SERVANTS.

A hound, now old, but one that for his master long
    had toiled;
One who in his earlier days by game was never
    foiled;
Worn out by weight of years, by toil, by trouble
    and decay,
Went with his master hunting the wild boar, joined
    in the race
And mingled in the sports of other days, the much-
    loved chase!

He boldly seized the boar, and fanged it in the ear,
When strength gave way, the boar escaped, caused
    by declining year:
Quick to him came the master, and angry said:
    "I'll thrash thee!"

The feeble dog replied: "Master, 'twas but my
    strength that failed me,
Not my will. Spare thy old servant! Remember me
    of yore!

Think of me as I was then, abuse not now, take
> pity, I implore!

"Oh, Master! many are the days for thee I've toiled
> when
Thou in poverty was struggling helpless as I was
> then!"
And faithful servants who have proven their merit
> many ways
All should remember well, and help in their declin-
> ing days!

THE DANCING KID.

Did you ever hear of the Dancing Kid
That strayed from the herd when its mother forbid?
Well, it left the fold on a summer's day
And determined to go away, away:
Away from its home in quest of fun,
For it was never content with the herd to run.

But there is many a pitfall — many a snare
To the young in life who are unaware;
Though brave and honest the girl or boy,
Life's full of vices that will destroy:
And the Dancing Kid was soon pursued
By a great old Wolf, which him subdued.

So there is many a victim allured by sin,
Deeming life but short, joins the hideous din;
And for a passing pleasure — a fleeting show —
Risks endless misery — eternal woe.
The Dancing Kid, deeming life but short,
Asked the Wolf's indulgence in a merry sport.

"If you pipe—I'll dance," said the Dancing Kid;
And the Wolf piped loud as he was bid;
His great jaws swelling as he blew entranced,
While the Dancing Kid, danced and danced:
As each sweet vibration rolled away
The Wolf did loud and louder play.

But the music was heard by Dogs hard by—
The Wolf growled these words, as he turned to fly:
"Who steps out of his way to play fool, is not wise,
And must never wonder if he loses the prize:
Like children who do what mothers forbid,"
A narrow escape had the Dancing Kid.

SPARE THE ROD AND SPOIL THE CHILD.

I can see King Solomon, seated upon Israel's throne,
Rich in lands, and gold, and jewels, with everything his own
That mortal man could ask or wish, that was upon the earth,
That surely would be calculated to give the king great mirth;
But wonder you, King Solomon, with his humanity,
Should exclaim, "Alas! alas! Vanity! All is vanity!"

Seven hundred wives had Solomon, of princely high degree,
I doubt if Mormon elder had more merry wives than he! [the king,
But his children acted dreadfully, and worried sore
To whip them well all 'round each day he thought the proper thing;
"Chasten thy son while there is hope, thy soul spare not his crying!"
Was a truth when Solomon wrote, perhaps there's no denying.

While this time-honored proverb, by Israel's greatest
    king,
Evidently was considered then quite the proper thing,
"Correct thy son, he shall give thee rest and delight
    thy soul!"
"The rod and reproof give wisdom!" his youth he
    might cajole,
But not a Yankee child to-day — away such nonsense
    wild,
At this most ancient maxim: "Spare the rod and
    spoil the child!"

Oh, how I used to dread it, in my youthful days
    gone by,
When every one would quote it, with blood right in
    their eye;
And with a tender feeling, akin to Beelzebub,
With a ferule or a hazel they viciously would drub;
And the music of the refrain, as it floated away in
    air,
Was but tears of simple childhood, which I was
    loath to bear!

A MERCILESS MIND.

Meeting a Lamb, when out walking one day,
Knowing the Lamb from its fold was astray,
A Wolf thus addressed him: "Hear, sir!
You grossly insulted me last year, sir!"
Bleated the Lamb, in mournful suspense:
"Indeed, you're mistaken, I had not come hence."

Then said the Wolf: "You feed on my clover,
A thing I've forbidden you over and over!"
Bleated the Lamb: "Your pasture's not wasted
For clover's a thing I never have tasted."
Again said the Wolf: "You drink from my well;
What the injury is I scarcely can tell."

"Mother's milk," said the Lamb. "is my food and
    my drink; [think."
I've not drank at your well; you're mistaken, I
"Ah," said the Wolf, "I cannot find plea
To eat him, that seemingly justifies me;
Still I'll seize him and eat him, although he refute
Everything, thus far, to him, I impute."

A wicked, tyrannical, merciless mind,
Some pretext for evil always will find.

A GUEST OF THE CLUB.

Exceedingly clever! and without any parade,
Wonderfully expert in handling a spade
In games, which he plays; while in wielding a club,
No one is more daring when playing the rub;
Then, in playing a hand, has hearts to command:
Few owning more diamonds than were held in his
    hand!
He is very convincing! Cards nestle about —
Make his acquaintance, should you have any doubt!

In dealing the cards, with a kindly regard
For himself, the game he will ofttimes retard;
And while the best of players are sitting close by,
In a manner mysterious, tho' sly;
Will obtain from the deck, cards almost a peck,
Proceeding his clothes to slyly bedeck!
And just how, when and where, he got those two
    pair,
Make the most of us secretly swear!

Then the bat of that eye! Delusive and sly,
You cannot ever catch it, nor can I;
'Tis convincing too late, as I witness our fate,
That most of our lives are predestinate!
Why, if some one would give us two dozen packs,
Neither you, nor could I, get more than two jacks;
Then, when he would call us! It would appall us
To meet the calamity which would befall us!

Sad are reflections! Many times I have wished,
When back in disgust my chair I have pushed,
That my eyes were not better at night —
As I would witness some brother's sad plight;
For none could keep pace with four kings and an
    ace —
Tho' stealing one king — a burning disgrace —
With a flush, he said was a "sequent"—
Which to me were amazingly frequent!

His raise of that blind was remarkably good,
As I quickly discovered after I stood!
Then the Doctor sat down, with face all aglow --
All doctors seem wise, even little they know —

Aching our hearts, our diamonds home sleeping,
Till the dawn of the morning's silently peeping.

Lovely's the morning — refreshing pure air;
The sun brightly beaming, new born, as it were;
But the sky may be clear, the morning serene,
Not so I fear one who rules home as a queen.
Oh, the thing that we dread is that gentle surprise —
Disguising our look — from her languishing eyes!
Have you experience? Aye, there is the rub
In staying out late with "A Guest of the Club."

TRANSFORMATION.

In the days of yore the gods possessed great power
    o'er all the clan,
They could change the bird into a beast, the beast
    into a man.
It is said the beasts in love became, as the instance
    which I cite,
Of a cat, that deeply fell in love, with man her
    fate to plight.

And she besought immediately, Venus, the goddess
    old —
Prayed to be transformed into a maid, to him her
    love unfold.
Venus, pitying, changed her form to that of a
    maiden fair,
With pearly teeth, and swan-like neck, and beautiful
    golden-hair.

Then quickly she sought her lover, as maidens have
    always done,
And won him with her beauty, as the maidens have
    ever won.

But their honeymoon was not over nor settled in a
 place,
When Venus said: "I've changed her form — of the
 cat is there a trace?"

While reclining in her chamber, with her lover by
 her side,
The lovely youth that she had won, now enamored
 of his bride —
Venus then let a little mouse drop at the maiden's
 feet —
She sprang from the bed in quick pursuit, intent to
 catch and eat!

When Venus again transformed her. "What's bred
 in the bone," she said,
"Will ever appear in the flesh, haven't I often
 read?"
"The cat, to a woman, I'll never transform — that's
 not my plan —
Its nature I'll give to woman, — and woman I'll give
 to man."

THE MAN OF DIGNITY.

Have you never seen him as he comes with solemn
    pace,
Proudly to the forum, in some important case,
Always sitting upright, with grave and serious mien,
Not seeming to augur usefulness — merely to be
    seen?
Giving to great occasions, both of Church and State,
By his august presence — simply pristine weight?

Aye, have you never seen him, sitting at the bar,
Stroking his big whiskers, looking graver far
Than any of his fellows, who, with jolly air,
Find a pleasure giving him the conspicuous chair!
Grandly he looks, majestic, while he rarely talks;
You discern his wisdom, as he sits or walks?

Ah, you have seen him, although you've never heard
Anything of greatness; he seldom says a word;
It is said, in speaking, he loses all that charm
That gently hangs about him, and shields the man
    from harm;

But their honeymoon was not over nor settled in a place,
When Venus said: "I've changed her form — of the cat is there a trace?"

While reclining in her chamber, with her lover by her side,
The lovely youth that she had won, now enamored of his bride —
Venus then let a little mouse drop at the maiden's feet —
She sprang from the bed in quick pursuit, intent to catch and eat!

When Venus again transformed her. "What's bred in the bone," she said,
"Will ever appear in the flesh, haven't I often read?"
"The cat, to a woman, I'll never transform — that's not my plan —
Its nature I'll give to woman, — and woman I'll give to man."

THE MAN OF DIGNITY.

Have you never seen him as he comes with solemn
    pace,
Proudly to the forum, in some important case,
Always sitting upright, with grave and serious mien,
Not seeming to augur usefulness — merely to be
    seen?
Giving to great occasions, both of Church and State,
By his august presence — simply pristine weight?

Aye, have you never seen him, sitting at the bar,
Stroking his big whiskers, looking graver far
Than any of his fellows, who, with jolly air,
Find a pleasure giving him the conspicuous chair!
Grandly he looks, majestic, while he rarely talks;
You discern his wisdom, as he sits or walks?

Ah, you have seen him, although you've never heard
Anything of greatness; he seldom says a word;
It is said, in speaking, he loses all that charm
That gently hangs about him, and shields the man
    from harm;

For this man of dignity can never bear the crosses
That fall to other men, without sustaining losses.

He ventures few opinions, lest those opinions might
Make his apparent wisdom become a little trite;
And you rarely ever see him try a hard-fought case,
For fear his seeming dignity he might thus efface;
But he adds a presence, and always holds the fort,
The most pompous personage that comes before the
    court.

VALOR.

A beautiful Fawn once said to a Stag,
Grown old and mischievous, given to brag,
Stamping his foot and shaking his head
Causing the herd considerable dread:
"Pray sire, are you not very large and strong?
Possessed of horns with many a prong?
Horns that are spreading — horns immense?
Horns that are useful in self-defence?
You have wind for either a race or jog,
You are swifter in running than the dog;
Then why is it, Stag? have you such fear,
When you see the hound, or his baying hear?

"O lovely Fawn!" said his Stagship old,
"Altho' to my herd I seem fierce and bold,
Altho' I'm vigorous and have skill,
Resolve with the hound to grapple at will,
To show my courage, and in future strife
Gore deeply the hound and take his life!

Demonstrate now and for all future time
Courage and valor while in my prime.
Ah! so soon as I hear the sound of his voice
Seemingly there is left no other choice;
My spirits fail, I cannot tarry me,
Off I go fast as my legs can carry me.

Argument to cowards no courage e'er gave —
Reason alone convinces the brave.

POLLY, YOU TALK TOO MUCH.

Polly was a bird well trained to talk,
Could mimic a whistle — anything mock;
Would scream at a dog; yell at the cat:
Away went Pussy when Poll cried "Scat!"
The dog would go at her words: "Come here!"
"Clear out, you rascal!" would run thro' fear.

But a spaniel dog, whose name was Mudge,
Was going down street with a stately trudge;
When Poll, on Mudge thinking a trick to play,
Spoke these words in a jocular way:
"Sic her, Mudge! Sic her!" as he passed her by —
"Sic, you ráscal, Sic!" — then turned to fly.

Mudge turned like a flash, as might be inferred,
And wiped the earth with that saucy bird.
It seemed that Poll would not hold together,
Or quit the fight with a single feather:
Tho' Mudge ran off when Poll cried "Get out!"
The life of the parrot was one of doubt.

Then hobbling up on some steps of stone,
With a bleeding wing and a broken bone;
She mused to herself, as well she might,
Regarding her conduct which brought the fight
"I think," said Poll, "this beats the Dutch,
Tho' the truth is, Polly, you talk too much!"

It was many a day ere Poll recovered,
'Twixt life and death for a long time hovered;
And when once more Poll was well and gay,
As she ate her cracker, strange words would say:
At least to the children they appeared as such,
When Poll would tell them: "Don't talk too much!"

THE SMILE OF WOMAN.

Life's pathway is thorned, tho' with roses adorned,
    The struggle is hard for man;
Yet cheerful he seems, and hardships he deems
    A part of God's wisdom and plan.
And thanks for the love of our Ruler above,
    Who gave one solace below,
Made earth's desert isle, by woman's sweet smile,
    A place even happy 'mid woe.

Hope ever beams bright, like a beacon light,
    Cheering us onward through life;
Not till gloom on us breaks, and sorrow o'ertakes,
    We falter and flee from earth's strife.
It is then woman's smile will ever beguile
    Sorrow away from man's heart;
May the day never dawn when her smile shall be
        gone,
    And we from it forever must part.

Life's shadows are cast, and on us fall fast,
    Like shades of the evening to stay;

And weary of strife, in the sunset of life,
    Man rests from the cares of the day.
Then, like lilies so fair, sun-kissed in the air,
    The smile of woman will leaven;
In the age of decline, when pressed by old Time,
    Woman makes life to us Heaven.

THE DISASTROUS CROSSING.

I hear complaint, that our neighbor's cow,
   That in venturing sees a passing train;
And in trying to make the crossing — how?
   In front of an engine — Alas, in vain!
For the engineer, in a reckless way
   Drives his engine — a deadly missile,
With the pilot catching any cow astray,
   Never ringing a bell or sounding whistle!
Why on McShane's crossing last Saturday night,
   Number Six, a passenger, two hours late,
Caught Smith's best Jersey, and killed outright
   His old milch cow with a loitering gait.

What a pity it is these trains won't stop
   For the old milch cow with a loitering gait;
That Knights of the Engine, with clubs don't hop
   And scare the cow — let passengers wait;
For time is nothing — Aren't the crossings free?
   Don't laws of the State permit cows to roam;

To eat up gardens, hook the maple tree;
   Ditch trains on crossings while coming home?
But what does it matter a train be thrown
   From off the track with its human freight;
A fireman killed, — a broken bone, —
   By the old milch cow with a loitering gait?

And what's it matter, — an engineer's fear;
   A passenger killed by this cruel fate;
That millions of property be lost each year
   By the old milch cow with a loitering gait.
The State still pastures this grand old cow;
   The streets and the crosses seem always free;
Roads, sidewalks, bridges — all subservient now
   To the old milch cow and her company;
Wouldn't the saving of millions, now spent in fence,
   Preventing the ditching of passengers, freights,
Be not a sufficient recompense,
   For keeping up cows with loitering gaits?

RECOMPENSE.

A Wolf, with a bone stuck fast in his throat,
Offered a Crane a twenty-pound note;
Promising pay, when the bone should be drawn
From the muscular throat of the Wolf so brawn.

  The long-necked Crane,
   For the love of gain,
Into his throat put her head so stout
And instantly drew the bone right out!

"Your money now," said the greedy Crane.
" I now have relieved you from all pain,
Surely sir! I want my reward?"
"Do you think," said the Wolf, "My word I regard?"

  His teeth ever winding
   'Mid grinning and grinding,
" You surely already have quite recompense
From the jaws of a Wolf your head to take hence."

A CHARIVARI.

The moon was rising, peeping through
    The lovely sky, with its azure blue;
For the hour was late, eleven had sped,
    Ere the guests and hosts retired to bed;
While the seeming stillness of the night,
    To the host and hostess gave delight.

The village boys before had heard,
    Joshua Judkins had caged a bird;
And the leader cried: "I'll put the question,
    Isn't a charivari, boys, a good suggestion?"
When out there rang in ringing notes,
    "Aye! aye!" from many lusty throats.

Said Jimmy McShane, the butcher's son,
    "I've a bucket of blood, hurrah for fun!
We'll pour it around the house, then see
    The cows give Joshua a charivari."
The blood was poured all over the grass,
    And the gates left open for cows to pass.

Brown's brindle cow was the first that bawled;
    Then her yearling heifer loudly called;
While fifty steers from Thompson's clover
    Threw down the fence and went rushing over;
The village cows furnished new recruits —
    A hundred strong, the bellowing brutes.

Joshua, from his nuptial bed did rouse,
    Hearing the noise of the bellowing cows,
In a garment red, with club quite stout,
    Fearlessly rushed to drive them out;
His good bride watching, yelled: "Murder, Fire!"
    As Joshua ran from their vengeful ire!

The cry was heard, by night-watchman caught—
    The cry of fire!—full of evil fraught;
And in night's stillness the fire bell rang,
    Its thundering clatter went Clang! clang! clang!
While neighbors ran in their clothes of night,
    As they only run in a panic's fright!

Meeting Jemmy as they rushing came,
    He bade them "stiddy!" there was no flame!

The bell was rung by some paltroon,
　　After welcomin' Joshua's honeymoon!
While the boys were on a bit of a spree;
　　And the cows were givin' a charivari!"

Again and again, was the sight unique,
　　As they pawed and bellowed in wild freak;
And assistance was of no avail
　　When a cow once struck the bloody trail!
They pawed and bellowed—tore the ground;
　　Bewailing the air with moaning sound!

Then, at the approach of the morning's light,
　　When the sun rose up, full, round, and bright;
The blood all covered, content to yield,
　　Each steer strolled back to his clover field.
Each cow went bawling home to her calf,
　　Leaving Joshua with his better half.

CAUTION.

A Ewe unto her darling said,
"Now, my Lamb, as you have been fed,
I'll take me hither to the mead,
And try to find myself some feed;
While I am gone, you watchful be
That harm may never come to thee."

"What shall I do, pray mamma dear,
When you are gone, if Wolves I hear?"
The mother said: "Ah, precious child,
Fear not the Wolves when roaming wild;
Stay in the fold, ope' not the door,
As I have told you oft before."

"But mamma, should a playmate come?"
"Do not answer, but be quite dumb;
Unless they give this watchword, fear —
'A curse on the Wolf, he may be near.'"
A Wolf was strolling by and heard —
Remembered well the Lamb's watchword.

The mamma gone, the Wolf came hence
To give the pass and make pretense;
"A curse on the Wolf, he may be near!"
Then to a crack he placed his ear.
"Ay sir, I hear the 'pass,' 'tis right;
Show now the 'sign,' 'A foot that's white.'"

The Wolf, without white feet, was astounded,
And went his way, somewhat confounded,
To think a Lamb would caution show,
Demanding "pass" and "sign" to know!
The Lamb in showing prudence rare,
Deprived the Wolf of mutton fare.

DISCONTENT.

Some timid Hares were in alarm;
In constant fear of coming harm;
Resolved one day in desperation
To rid themselves of all vexation.
"Enemies will each day annoy;
And snares will be set us to decoy;
Or else by hounds we'll be pursued;
Our helpless race will be subdued."

The leader did to all propose
A way to rid themselves of woes;
"We'll to a precipice all go
And jump into the lake below."
So off they started, running fast —
Each leap was made like 'twere the last —
Each Hare to seek a watery grave —
Life's troubles bury 'neath the wave.

Upon the banks a school of Frogs,
With scarce a care, on sunny logs,

Heard their approach with great affright,
And each one jumped with all his might —
Into the bottom of the lake,
As quick as legs could bodies take.
"Hold up!" cried the leading Hare,
Our case is not one of despair!

" For here are others more faint-hearted
That by our running we have started!
We'd best not do as first intended!"
So back each Hare his own way wended:
Finding more timid creatures sent
On earth, the Hares were more content
To wrestle with the cares of life:
For each doth daily have his strife.

LABOR HAS ITS REWARD.

A Heifer was watching an Ox one day,
   When the Ox was hard at work;
While the Heifer was bounding about at
      play
   She would frequently laugh and smirk.

And taunt the Ox with reflections
   On his very unhappy fate:
In being compelled to labor
   From early until late.

Shortly after was the harvest home:
   Then the owner the Ox released:
While the Heifer was bound with strong
      cords,
   To be slain at the harvest feast.

The Ox said unto the Heifer,
   As her owner drove her away:
"For this you were in idleness
   So long allowed to stay:

I've noticed one thing all my life
  The idle may flourish awhile;
But an evil day will take them away —
  Good-bye!" said the Ox, with a smile.

Then let us always remember,
  And thro' life it always regard :
There is no one thing truer here on earth —
  Than, "Labor has its reward."

IN CONTEMPT.

Into a trial court, by chance, one day,
Two Irish gentlemen did idly stray;
His Honor was calling a case between
Timotheus Smith versus John McQueen.
Counselor Jennings, with a bald old pate,
Began the jury to interrogate;
First, tendering four, to Counselor Clair,
Whose shining cranium was minus hair.

"Arrah! Ted," said Pat, to his Irish mate,
"Be the powers that be—these men ornate,
Who're tryin' the case, are wather scald;
Fa'th! the skelps o' the lawyers both are bald!
I'll bet"—"Order! gentlemen," roared the judge;
"Orther!" cried Pat, giving Teddy a nudge.
"Bring up the culprits before the court!"
"What fer, Yer Honor?" was the quick retort.

"Let a fine be entered for contempt!"
"Contimpt? Why! Yer Honor, 'twas
    niver drimpt!
I was merely offerin' my brother Ted,
To wager a bit on the lawyer's head;
Whin, Yer Honor, yers'lf did fret an' frown
I was goin' to put five dollars down
That the bald-headed lawyer would win
    the case,
Divil I'll bet—if it offinds Yer Grace."

FLATTERY.

An old thievish Crow, devoid all fear,
Had stolen cheese from a cottage near,
The dainty morsel the Fox could see
As the Crow flew over into a tree.
"Well!" said the Fox, "I humbly confess,
Cheese is a thing I'd love to possess;
But how to succeed I hardly know
Unless it be to flatter the Crow."

Then he exclaimed: "How handsome the Crow!
In beauty no bird where'er I go
Will excel her! In form perfection!
The fairest of fair her complexion!
But oh, what a horrid, horrid voice!
If it equaled her beauty, Crow's choice
Of all the birds for a ruling queen,
For the Crow's a bird fine as I've seen!"

The foolish Crow, anxious to refute
Reflections cast by the wily brute;
Then let go her cheese, and, la, la, la!
Began an unearthly, "Caw, caw, caw!"
Snapping it up: "It is quite a meal
For a hungry Fox, better I feel;"
"And good Crow," said the Fox, now taunting,
"Your voice is good, but wit is wanting!"

It is well, dear friends, by this to see
A flatterer lives on flattery,
And will flatter not, without some aim;
And should you heed him, who is to blame?
The Crow was quite slow to comprehend
Between a real and pretended friend;
And hungry went — that day was living
On fulsome praise the Fox was giving.

INTEGRITY.

A thief one night came to a yard,
   A house to break for booty,
But found the House-Dog, there a guard
   Intent on doing duty.
"Here, fellow," throwing him some meat,
   "Come here, sir! Stop your alarm.
Fine old Dog! Why do you not eat?
   Why bark? Sir, I mean no harm."

"This sudden kindness, sir, of yours,
   These favors unexpected,
To one who guards his master's doors,
   Must promptly be rejected.
Ah, sir! you have some private ends
   To accomplish for your gain.
On integrity all depends;
   To betray, sir, I disdain."

Oft in this life it is the case,
   We have a place of trust and care,

There's nothing more will us disgrace
   Integrity then to spare!
'Tis pleasure gone at heavy cost —
   Betraying trusts when given,
Respect of all on earth we've lost, —
   And worthless sure for heaven!

BEST LOOK BEFORE YOU LEAP.

A Fox which fell into a well,
    Was casting all about;
For 'twas quite hard for him to tell
    Just how he should get out.

A Goat came to the well and stood
    Wanting a little drink,
Asked Reynard: "Was the water good?"
    And, "Plenty did he think?"

Said Fox, dissembling his sad plight;
    "Come down, my friend, and see;
"I think 'twould give you much delight,
    'Tis cool as it can be."

Down leaped the Goat, head, horns and all;
    The Fox jumped on him quick;
Out of the well, over the wall,
    Was now a simple trick.

Then spake the Fox: "Had you the brains
    You have of woolly beard,

You would be often spared the pains
  Leaping at what you heard!"

"For life's at best a constant steep!
  'Tis hard to climb, who can?
Then, always look before you leap
  Is much the wiser plan!"

HELP.

Once a youthful bather
   Bathing in the sea,
Called to a traveler:
   "Oh, come save me!"

For the little bather
   Was going down, down, down;
Down to feed the fishes;
   To drown, drown, drown!

Very unconcernedly
   Stood the traveler there,
Telling the little bather:
   "Of water to beware!"

"It very imprudent was,
   Unless that he could swim;
To go into deep water —
   That much he'd say to him!"

"Oh, sir!" cried the bather,
   "Help, help me! ere I go;

You may scold me ever after—
　　But save me now from woe!"

The traveler him admonished;
　　The boy sunk out of sight;
And was never more permitted
　　Again to see the light:

So I say that counsel
　　Without help's of little use;
When one needs a helping hand
　　Words are a poor excuse.

MOLLITER MANUS IMPOSUIT.

A client to his lawyer said
Another had with club his head
Pounded and beaten on his skull,
Until his senses all were dull.
And hence, to have his wrongs corrected,
As well as all his rights protected,
He merely now had called to see
The law's appropriate remedy.

The lawyer quickly glanced to look
And took from off his shelf a book;
Then with his pen began to write,
These words on paper did indite:
John Smith, the plaintiff, here complains
Of James Jones, defendant, and maintains
That on, etc., with force and arms
Defendant perpetrated, to wit, harms.

He violently seized the plaintiff's hair,
Then pulled and tore till scalp was bare;

Then with his fists struck many blows,
Resulting in a bunged-up nose;
Then having downed him with a brick,
He did the plaintiff kick and kick;
The damage done to shirt and collar,
Was of the value of one dollar.

By means which, the plaintiff hurt and
    bruised,
Sick, sore and lame, thus badly used,
Physician's bill he has incurred,
One hundred dollars is averred;
And other wrongs, to plaintiff, great,
As well, the people of the State,
Wherefore, the plaintiff, injured, sues—
One thousand will his wrongs excuse.

First plea: Not guilty; Second: 'tis said
Molliter manus imposuit, was plead,
That is, defendant but gently laid
His hands upon the plaintiff, and him
    stayed

From striving with force and arms to beat
His neighbor Green in passion's heat;
The plaintiff's trespasses above narrated,
He verifies were those here stated.

Then to the jury did each counsel show
Defendant's zeal and plaintiff's woe;
Then to the jury plaintiff's counsel came
And said: Defendant, by his plea, admits
   his blame;
Molliter manus imposuit was the plea,
Filed by the counsel, let it translated be:
Molliter, he mauled, *manus*, the man, to wit,
My client, and on him imposed — *imposuit.*

HYPOCRISY.

A Wolf, bitten by dogs, wounded, lay
   In his lair almost asleep:
When, perchance, a Sheep astray,
   Into the lair did peep.

"Maimed sorely I am, my friend --
   The fever running high tide --
Pray fetch me some water, and then
   Myself with meat I'll provide."

"A fine idea!" the Sheep replied;
   "If I should bring you the draught
I for you, too, meat will provide,
   The instant I am caught.

Looks deceitful avoid,
   And hypocritical speech,
If never by these annoyed
   Life's highest stations you'll reach.

THE FARMER'S SOLILOQUY.

The autumn days are upon us,
  The leaves look yellow and sear;
And cold chilly winds that blow on us
  Make a fellow feel shaky and queer.
But the corn's full ripe and resplendent,
  With ears 'most as big as cordwood;
And crops upon which we're dependent,
  This year are uncommonly good.

And the stock is all fat in the pasture,
  For the rains that came down cleared away
The drouth, that had weighed with disaster,
  Giving the chinz bug carnival sway:
Aye, thanks to the rain that descended,
  And grew up the vine and the gourd;
Things this season are happily blended,
  And God blessings upon us has poured.

And turkeys! Why, gobblers are struttin'
  Everywhere up and down the lot,

Never dreaming Christmas will be puttin'
    Them on to our tables hot!
The potatoes are placed in the cellar,
    Tomatoes and berries all canned;
With apples, the finest, and meller;
    That ever were raised in the land!

The farmer ought to be happy,
    If you let him alone he will;
And while his corn may be sappy,
    There's plenty in every hill.
But it seems like trusts and combines.
    The tariff. jute plant, and all,
With freights so extortionate sometimes,
    The farmer goes to the wall!

AN EPISODE.

She cried, and O her tears, how sweet!
Her handsome form was trim and neat.
When asked the reason of the fuss,
Her only answer was, "That Gus!"

O speak! I said — an answer came —
"No, no sir! little he's to blame.
A kiss, he stole, it was no muss —
I cried, forsooth, because that Gus — "

I said again, "A stolen kiss
From such a fair and handsome miss,
Is battery in the first degree!"
Her answer, — "What! Gus kissing me?"

Quoth I to her, "He well doth know,
A stolen kiss is but a blow.
A grave offence, I'd fine, as judge!"
Her sweet reply to me was, "Fudge!"

LUXURY AND EASE.

O Luxury, I long for thee!
And beckon Ease come live with me—
   Then will I be content!
There's little else man wants below,
Few will ever that little know—
   'Tis Heaven's choice blessing sent.

'Tis not a luxury I crave,
In indolence and wealth to lave—
   A life I would deplore;
For bonds, nor gold, lull not to rest
The anguish of a troubled breast,
   Nor bring content in store.

Not for the ease of idle thought
Which wealth hath its possessor taught,
   Longs now my heart, nor sighs;
But O the Ease I long to taste
Is with content to be well graced,
   Such, treasure never buys.

Aye, fawning man! thy sordid mind
In pomp of power expects to fiud
   True ease and rich repose.
'Tis only when thy cup is filled,
With bitter dregs life has distilled,
   The emptiness then shows.

The tallest oak must bend and break
Before the storms that will o'ertake,
   Though seeming ever strong;
The proudest warrior in his power
Will crumble like the castle's tower—
   Be silent dust ere long.

Ah, Luxury and Ease, I ween
Comes from a happy go between—
   Seek not to emulate
The one who thirsts alone for Fame,
For Gold, or an Undying Name—
   Have pity for such fate!

Aye, happiness you'll find most dear,
If found in life, is always near,

No matter where you roam;
You seek for Ease in distant climes;
And Luxury in propitious times —
To find them at thy Home.

ALLIE.

Last night, in dreams, I saw her face,
    Her darling form to me was near;
Her beauty, charms and lovely grace
    Brought to my eyes a gladsome tear.

Allie, I thought, was with me there,
    And our two hearts beat now as one,
In bliss and happiness we were
    From twilight until morning's sun.

In childish sports we mingled o'er,
    And we of Nature's sweets partake;
She was to me the same as yore,
    I loved her for love's own sweet sake.

'Twas but a dream that to me came—
    A fleeting dream—'tis come! 'tis fled!
Would I were yet in bliss the same,
    With my lost Allie dear, instead.

THE LITTLE PHYSICIAN.

There is no type of man
Among all I can scan,
Assumes such a mystical air,
As the little physican —
A kind of magician —
A man of some unction, as 'twere.

He is always quite dapper,
Remarked as a snapper,
Important in the superlative degree;
And when called to a case,
Assumes such a wise face,
You are struck with the wisdom you see!

Polite, to a fault,
He bows should you halt,
And tips a small hat which he wears;
With his pill-bags and cane,
Tho' seemingly vain,
'Tis only his knowingsome airs.

When he visits the ill,
With powder and pill,
Prescribes for a patient with brains;
His bump of conceit
Is the first thing you meet,
As you lie there, racking with pains.

As an expert, I ween,
No other I've seen,
Can theorize in, and then out;
A hypothetical case,
He states with such grace,
As convinces beyond reasonable doubt.

But his faults are all laid,
Where the willow's deep shade
Obscures them forever from view,
As you pause to reflect,
And can only suspect
The devil will some day get his due.

For there's no type of man
Among all I can scan,

Assumes such a mystical air,
    As the little physician —
    A kind of magician —
A man of some unction, as 'twere.

WHAT IS LIFE?

Is life not an empty bubble;
   But an iridescent dream?
Only a wave of trouble
   Pushing man along the stream?

Is life real, or a fancy spell
   To men mortal given,
That teaches to abhor a hell,
   And to adore a heaven?

Can it be said the daily task
   Of mortals here below,
If 'twere exposed without a mask
   Would many pleasures show?

Will not the toiler for his bread,
   Who bends the same each day,
Still have the same enduring dread
   Of starvation's debt to pay?

'Tis ever toil, and ever strife,
   From morn until the sun

Closes the evening of our life,
   And Man his race has run!

Yet, still this life is full of Hope,
   And he who battles strong,
Is able with the world to cope —
   Happy as he goes 'long.

'Twas made, that we might toil and plan
   For our existence here,
God will reward the struggling man —
   Let each be of good cheer.

MY MARY.

My Mary is a charming girl,
   I will not underrate her;
So fair is she that a' the rest
   Wi' spite and envy hate her.

O deep is an artesian well,
   And deeper yet the ocean;
Still deeper in my bosom is
   My love and my devotion.

I'll gather daisies in the spring,
   To glad her heart with flowers;
On leafy trees the birds will sing,
   While we sit 'neath the bowers.

The honey-bee still sips and sips
   The honey frae the rose,
But I ha' found upon her lips
   Far sweeter honey grows.

'Tis her I wish some day to wed,
　My darling little fairy;
The violets blue and roses red
　I'll pluck and gie my Mary.

CHANGES.

To think the changes that take place,
    What time will bring around;
You look now on some boyish face —
    The future man of town.

Some boy who once was very poor,
    Fortune, the fickle Dame,
Knocks at his splendid mansion door,
    And tells us of his fame!

And Fortune whispers with joy and pride,
    In accents clear and loud:
"Should my favors be on your side,
    Be thou not vain nor proud.

"For humble yet thy lot may grow;
    Act wisely every day;
And learn a lesson; 'tis well to know
    That Fortune may fly away!

"Just think how few are the people left
   We mingled with of yore;
How many families now bereft
   That ne'er knew grief before!

"And think how time will Fortune change,
   All things, and people, too;
O'er all the universal range
   Things change, and so will you."

THREE PLAGUES.

Regret for the past! why, have none!
    Best banish dull care away;
For the past is gone, all that is done
    Is with us ever to stay.

Grief, at the present! O tell me,
    Will it do a whit of good?
Earth's happiness we can all see
    Ever present if we would.

Anxiety, for the future!
    I merely wish to suggest,
Life's sorrows we only nurture
    That misery be our guest.

Three plagues of human existence!
    Expel them all from the mind;
'Twill help and be of assistance
    The pleasures of life to find.

TO PORTIA.

Sweet little girl, thy tender years
Are now thine own, but soon one hears
   The call to a maturer life:
But for thee we have little fears;
   Life will be one of joy — not strife.

To be happy, this life endears —
Women I find our best compeers —
I trust thou'll some day be a wife,
     Sweet little girl.

For there is nothing life so cheers,
   As the sweet wives we call our dears,
   Earth's pleasures then are rife:
And fame divine which one reveres
   Will be far sweeter in this life,
     Sweet little girl.

DAUNT NOT THE SPIRIT.

Daunt not the spirit,
    Let it be free
As the winds that sweep
    O'er land and sea!

Crush not the spirit,
    O let it roam,
Free as the waves
    On ocean home!

Cage not the spirit,
    Let it run wild,
Like to a laughing
    Wayward child!

Bind not the spirit,
    O let it soar
Always heavenward
    Toward Hope's bright star!

Spirit of Mortal,
  Ever be proud!
From day of thy birth
  Till wrapt in the shroud.

FORGIVE, O THAT RELIGION!

Forgive, O that religion
    That teaches one to hate,
A wandering, wayward brother
    That seeks thro' another gate!

God help them to hold up in faith;
    Forgive—it is a rarity;
The only strength they have is—Hope,
    They've naught of Christian charity.

To God and man alike unjust,
    They will their brothers wrong,
"Not in Thee alone" have they put their trust,
    E'en tho' their prayers be long.

They at the stake would gladly burn
    Those differing from their view;
O God, we trust thou wilt in turn
    Love and forgive them too.

TO MARY.

Sweet woman, let me here confess
    The love I have for thee;
A while no more thy lips I'll press—
    Still wilt thou think of me?

My Mary, thou canst not forget
    Glad times we've had together,
Dear are they to my memory yet,
    And dear will be forever.

'Twas love, so gentle, kind and true,
    The love that never dies;
The while I bid thee now adieu,
    Thy love I'll ever prize.

TEMPORAL POWER.

On a roof standing
A Kid was bandying
Words with a Wolf passing by:
And began to defile him,
To taunt and revile him,
Feeling quite safe up so high.

Said the Wolf: "Thee I hear,
And thy cowardly jeer,
But nothing you say doth me shock;
'Tis the place where you stand—
If I had you in hand,
Not long, sir, me would you mock!"

It is often the case,
There's advantage in place,
And also in temporal power;
One must not abuse it,
Nor ever misuse it,
But try and make every hour

A remembrance spot,
Which memory will not
Forget, but ever will treasure;
Or else you'll disgrace
Not only the place,
But yourself, likewise, in a measure.

WHAT IS THERE BETTER MAN CAN DO?

What is there better man can do
   Than lead a Christian's life;
The vices of this world eschew—
   Its never ending strife?
Ah, it is sweet to work for heaven,
   And do the Master's will,
For God will all our sorrows leaven,
   His promises fulfill.

It is sublime for man to work
   Like the Savior of his kind,
And never from life's duties shirk,
   But try more good to find;
To ever try the good to teach,
   That men may better grow,
And by kind deeds their hearts to reach,
   God's saving grace to know.

'Tis noble then each day to give
   The time, the thought, the care,

So long as God gives life to live
   To fight the tempter's snare.
The good we do in life will be
   A credit to our soul;
The man of good will ever see —
   God will His deeds enroll.

TRUE MIGHT.

Boasting, the North Wind said to the Sun:
  "Never by you will I be outdone;
I am more powerful and will try
  Who shall be victor—you or I."

"Then," said the Sun, "this I propose,
  I will use warmth and you may use
    blows,
On yonder traveler, and we'll try
  Whether you can first strip his cloak
    or I."

Then blew the North Wind a vigorous
    blast,
  The shivering traveler held his cloak
    fast;
The strong North Wind failed after an
    hour
  To remove the cloak by might or power.

Beaming out brightly the Sun then shone
  In genial warmth from his royal throne;
No longer cold, the man cast in delight
  The cloak the Wind failed to remove
      by might.

And from that time to the present day
  A kind, gentle manner, best will pay;
Persuasion is better than use of force,
  A manner humane the wiser course.

Tears of affection are precious things;
  Tears of subjection sure sorrow brings;
Tears of force to the eyes of sorrow
  Bring never a joy for the bright to-
      morrow.

DISCRETION.

'Twas summer hot,
The lake was not
Deep water for a home;
'Twould soon go dry,
'Twas best to hie —
Two froggies thought to roam.

So off they went
On water bent,
And searched all o'er the plain;
When soon they found
A well, large round,
The sun could never drain.

"Into it plump,
Come, let us jump!
It is delicious, cool!
'Tis not good wit,
Just wait a bit!"
Said the other: "Deep's the pool!

If it were dry
With walls so high,
How could we e'er get out?
We'd better stay
In the lake; some day
'Twill rain beyond a doubt."

'Tis sense, I think
When on the brink
Of a danger-threatening place,
When peril's great,
Never to wait,
But quick one's steps retrace.

SUMMER'S LABOR.

One cold, frosty day,
An Ant ate away
On food which we may
   Gather in summer
When we feel well and gay.

A Grasshopper, half fed,
From hunger nigh dead,
Besought her for bread:
   "When 'tis not summer
'Twas a hard life he lead."

"What were you doing?
What trade pursuing?
Why were you not viewing
   The fields of the summer
For the winter ensuing?"

Said the Grasshopper gay:
"I danced every day,
And was singing alway,

Thinking the summer
Would forever here stay."

Said the Ant, cheerily:—
Singing then merrily—
"This I say, verily:
Who labors not summer,
Winters pass drearily."

DISSENSION.

Four Bulls were calmly feeding
    Upon the summer's grass;
A Lion lay in ambush
    Waiting to make a pass.

But while they fed together,
    He would not make them prey;
They guarded well each other
    And cared not to estray.

The Lion at last succeeded
    In making an aversion;
By jealousy he breeded
    In causing a dispersion.

Then when the Bulls were separate
    And from each other gone,
'Twas easy to annihilate
    And eat them one by one.

'Tis ever thus dissensions will,
Among the best of friends,
Breed nothing good, but only ill—
On peace success depends.

MY LADY FAIR.

Entwine thy hair, my lady fair,
   With roses off the lea;
The dewy rose that fragrant grows
   To glad thy heart and me.
Upon its stem a diadem
   So lustrous to behold;
Though sweet indeed upon the mead,
   Sweet in thy hair of gold.
Then deck thy hair—these roses rare
   Seem fit and gay for thee;
In beauty glows the lovely rose
   I'll pluck and bring to thee.

O! golden hair, that will compare
   With the mermaids of the sea;
O! starlit eyes, 'mid sunny skies,
   Where wealth and beauty be!
Thou dost beguile, with radiant smile,
   By thy beauteous self I swear,

Thy wealth of bliss I will not miss,
　　But seek and with thee share.
Then will I twine, O lady mine,
　　About thy golden hair
The fairest rose the heather grows,
　　To deck thee, lady fair.

SCOTCH LETTER.

The wind is blawing very cauld.
As now my paper I enfauld
To write unto my ain dear hame,
Wi' mony a wish you're blest in same.
I'm very well, and God be thankit,
I'm able, as of auld, to shankit.
Sometimes I'm happy wi' my lot,
Sometimes I'm sad—why, I wot not;
But still it gi'es me greatest joy
To wat I'm Mither's darlin' boy.
I read an' write a' the day long,
Blackstone, Metcalf, an' syne a song;
O'er Tam O'Shanter I laugh by turns,
Wrote by the poet Robert Burns.
I hae na wife, I hae na dame,
God grant I ne'er may hae the same:
For I'm content to live alone—
Mony's the troubles then I'll shun —
Then ilka day, and ilka hour
That I hae time and hae the power;

To write shall be my greatest ettle—
Ah, gin I o'ly hae the mettle.
But to my letter, I hae left it,
An' a' the gither wandered frae it;
Na mair I dare na trifle wi' you,
Sic clish-ma-claver as I do gie you,
I ken, does bother auld folks greatly;
I'll ask, is she still proud an' stately,—
My wordy beast, my weel gaun filly?
There ne'er was better than auld Mollie.
Oh denna keep her poor and knaggie,
Gie meikle corn to her auld baggie;
Wi' fond caress on mony a day,
Gie to her meikle oats an' hay.
Mayst thou hae meikle to eat an' drink,
An' aye enough o' needfu' clink.
An' neist, how is my bonny sister?
God bless her an' her guid auld mither—
An' also bless her guid auld daddie—
I'll bless ye a', your bonnie laddie.
To a', my everlastin', never dyin'—
An' sure, I canna keep frae cryin',

For as I write, I ken one other
I'd rather see, than meet her brother,
Who lives awa' in our auld town,
For a better one canna be foun'—
In bonnie boys it aye surpasses;
In comely maids, an' bonnie lasses.
Sinna I canna be wi' you,
Be happy still as I bid adieu;
An' if I should be slee an' funny,
Pray think o' me, your ain guid sonnie;
An' of'en write me a guid auld letter,
Naught there is will please me better;
Careless is he who aye postpones—
Remember
        Yours truly,
                Will C. Jones.

CRAFTY.

A Fox, who never a Lion
   Had seen until that day,
Crouched meekly with fear before him,
   In a fearfully frightened way.

But upon a second meeting
   He'd lost some of his fright,
And talked with the Lion boldly,
   As if it were a right.

At his third visit, emboldened,
   He to the Lion said:
"When first I saw a Lion
   I had an awful dread;

But I find from close acquaintance —
   I often see and hear,
With those we term the mighty,
   That greatness flees when near.

And familiarity breeds, sir,
   Contempt, likewise, I know."
"Begone!" said the Lion; "villain!
   Crafty, as well as low."

THE FIRESIDE.

I love to sit by the winter's fire,
And enjoy its warmth to my heart's desire,
With life's affairs no more perplext,
In my favorite book I peruse the text—
The lord of a castle all my own,
And as glad as a king on his royal throne.

To the cheerful blaze come merry souls,
With faces bright as the glowing coals.
Too soon these ties the years may sever,
And those we love may be gone forever.
The ties of home are more dear to me
Than anything else in life I see.

The winds may whistle around the roof;
From the chilling storms I can keep aloof;
And I look about for the near and dear;
And feel and know that we all are here.
There is naught in life to me but this—
The sweet content of domestic bliss.

The pleasures of home let us all enjoy!
With its innocent gladness your time em-
 ploy!
For life is fleeting -- a passing breath;
The young and the old soon fall in death.
Of the pleasures of life we ask but this —
The sweet content of domestic bliss.

CHRISTMAS.

I still love to think of scenes like this,
   Of days now long since gone;
When I was a child in my hallowed bliss,
   A boy—an only one.
On Christmas eve my stockings were hung—
"Old Santa" was sure to come;
And merry hearts made merry tongue,
   And we were all at home.

Those days are past and I a boy
   Older in years have grown;
Yet still, when I think, it gives me joy
   To know them once my own!
I am far from home this Christmas day,
   Where I but meet and bow,
No friends I greet — I'm sick and away —
   Christmas is lonely now.

I think of it all — here every word —
   The circle is formed, I know;

By merry hands the fire is stirred —
  I see its cheerful glow.
Think they of me? I am with them there
  In the midst of Christmas rings,
Tho' I feel the sting of a silent tear
  My lonely Christmas brings.

I am thinking now, yes, thinking now,
  Of distant pleasure climes;
Plighting myself in a silent vow
  For future Christmas times!
The time speeds slow; O! my heart's distress!
  On this long, lonely day —
Yet I wile me away from its dreariness
  Thinking of friends far away.

AN ILL-SORTED LEAGUE.

A Mouse, on one ill-omened day,
    Made the acquaintance of a Frog,
When, after making a short stay,
    They started off upon a jog.

The Frog he feigned a great affection
    To keep his friend the Mouse from harm;
And urged it was for her protection
    To have her tied unto his arm.

When, coming nigh unto a brook,
    The Frog said: "Come, have courage, swim,"
And with a plunge the Frog then took
    The frightened Mouse in after him.

The Mouse went floundering about,
    And did a great commotion make;
Until a kite, them spying out,
    Concluded both of them to take.

And pouncing down she caught the Mouse,
  Thus tied so tightly to the Frog,
And bore them from their watery house,
  And straightway ate them on a log.

Ill-matched alliance always end
  Just like that of the Frog and Mouse.
For none who read will e'er contend
  Two such as they could keep one house.

And one who will his neighbor trap,
  Or foully set for him a snare,
Will find himself in some mishap
  Before he fully is aware.

AN ILL-FORMED ALLIANCE.

A Lion roaming on the pebbly shore
    Espied a Whale on the surface basking,
And calling to him in a loud roar,
    Began these questions asking:

"As I am the king of the lands,
    And you the king of the seas,
Would it not be proper that we join hands
    And have power to do as we please?"

The Whale to assent to this seemed glad,
    And promised with right good will,
For neither of them a doubt then had
    He couldn't his promises fulfill.

It chanced the Lion was first in a fight,
    Attacking a Bull one day,
And he called to the Whale with all his might,
    To take the Bull's gores away.

The Whale would gladly have joined in
    the fray,
But he was unable to leave the sea,
Tho' the Lion his friend he would not be
    tray,
  Yet he proved but a poor ally to be.

It is best when you form any compact,
    On the land or on the sea,
That all of the parties to the act
    Are able and will all agree.

And then, too, before the contracting,
    Be careful — make no mistake —
That both the contracting parties
    Can do all they undertake.

DECEPTION.

A wealthy Roman, in days of yore,
Oft for his friends had good in store;
Sometimes it was a feast, sometimes a show
To which his neighbors were asked to go.
One day he proffered a large reward
To him who offered the fittest card—
That is, to him who would play best—
Amuse the people by joke or jest.

Contesting artists began to arrive,
Each with the other soon to strive;
Incited by eagerness for the prize,
Each tried his best to seem most wise.
Reports went round, the neighbors flocked
Until the Forum fairly rocked
With eager people, there to see
Conjurers of such high degree.

A Mountebank gave out, one day,
That he had something new to play;

Something which he would vouch no age
Had yet produced on any stage:
Amid curiosity and suspense,
Without assistants, stepping hence;
He mimicked a pig, so like the squeal
The audience thought the pig quite real.

Some said the pig was 'neath his cloak,
And claimed the trick to be a joke.
Others insisted upon a search,
Intent the clever trick to smirch.
They searched the showman — searched
    him well —
And to the audience they would tell
That nothing upon him could be found.
Applause went high, round after round.

A Farmer 'mongst his neighbors sat,
Observed the trick not new, and that
He could perform in better style,
Which caused his fellows but to smile.
The morrow came, with it the crowd,
All ready with their praises loud

Of Mountebank, who stepping front,
Would mimic both the squeal and grunt.

Up went the hands of the audience all,
Cheer after cheer that would appall
The Farmer, who began to feel
For ears of a pig that was real.
He pinched the ears and pulled the tail,
And the pig to squeal would never fail;
While the audience hissed at every sound,
Until the squeal was fairly drowned.

"Romans, I see you love deceit,
Discard the real for the cheat;
Applaud the mimic of the squeal,
And hiss at the one you know is real."
Then, much to everyone's surprise,
He placed the pig before their eyes.
And do not we who live to-day
Conduct ourselves in the Roman way?

LIFE'S GRAPES.

Ripe, lovely grapes, but trellised high,
   A roving Fox by chance did spy;
And as they hung in a sunny glow
   They were to the Fox a tempting show.
Reynard by many a vain leap tries
   To get a taste of the longed-for prize,
But finding possession quite out of his power,
   Said: "It matters not; the grapes are sour."
So the grapes of life, which ofttimes we
   So dearly covet whenever we see,
But finding them beyond our reach,
   Like the sly old Fox, "sour grapes" we preach.

THE MISER.

All that he had a Miser sold,
Receiving therefore a lump of gold.
    Which he buried away
    Where it wouldn't pay,
    Into a hole that very day.
It was a very secluded spot,
At least that is what the Miser thought —
    By the side of a wall,
    Once stately, tall,
    But demolished all,
Scattering a pile of sand and brick —
No better place could a Miser pick.

Daily the Miser went that way,
Frequent his visits, short his stay;
    And it was his delight
    To know it was tight
    In a hole out of sight —
Away under the ground, safe and sound
From mercenary people tramping 'round.

For in a measure
His only pleasure
Was in this treasure.
And none can tell what the Miser thought,
Or the heavenly joy this treasure brought.

A little caution I would advise,
Tho' extra caution's not overwise;
Was the thief's thought
Who marked the spot
And formed a plot
To dig into the Miser's treasure,
Then carry it away at pleasure,
At dead of night,
When there was no light
To mark his flight.
It was thought to be cunning, crafty, bold —
The way the Miser lost his gold.

At his next visit the Miser found
Naught but a hole — a hole in the ground
Then he tore his hair,
In his great despair,

And sorrow there.
Imagine a lifetime's pleasure lost!
Then think of the trouble this treasure cost.
    Oh, wretched man!
    More miserable than
    All earthly clan!
And the Miser wished that he was dead,
For the joys of life for him had fled.

A friend found him cast down with grief,
And ministered thus to his relief:
    "Pray, why dost grieve?
    Sir, by your leave,
    A stone I'll heave
Into the hole, you may fancy gold —
'Twill answer your purpose at least ten-
    fold."
    For you are aware,
    When your gold was there,
    The only care
Was its safety — not its use to lend —
Then a stone is a thing you cannot spend."

But the Miser in life no more joy found;
Soon died and was buried in the ground,
    Without oration,
    Without ovation,
    By the donation
Of some kind friends — there were but few
Who in his lifetime the Miser knew.
    His grave so lone
    Now bears a stone,
    With words his own :
"Miserable! Miserly! Heed, my friend —
For the wants of life your money spend."

THE REWARD OF STEALTH.

Reynard was blessed with a bushy tail,
Of lovely hair he was wont to trail—
   No other's was more graceful.
He thought he had unbounded wit—
At least a plenty to care for it,
   And carried it quite graceful.
But people will always a thief abhor,
And against them wage continual war.

Reynard kept stealing, year after year,
The neighborhood poultry without fear,
   That justice would o'ertake him.
He would prowl by night and sneak by day,
Gobbling up chickens that came in his way,
   Thinking luck would not forsake him.
But Reynard staying out one night quite late,
Met this, a most untimely fate.

Reynard, while stealing, fell into a trap,
And tho' full of vigor and full of snap,

Energy was of no avail.
Serious trouble! His thoughts came quick,
Only one remedy — cut off slick
   His beautiful bushy tail.
Sensible he was to this disgrace,
Sensible too of the time and place.

Resolving, however, to make the best
Of a matter bad, he said to the rest:
   "Foxes, it is with joy I hail
The convenience with which I move about,
I feel quite at ease, and should you doubt,
   Do away with your bushy tail."
But scorn and laughter were heaped upon
The unfortunate Fox when he had done.

OPPRESSION.

A Wolf stole down on a shepherd's fold,
    And seized a Lamb, in a manner bold,
And began to bear it off to his lair,
    Intent upon making a meal of it there;
When a Lion, switching his tail in wrath,
    Suddenly leaped across his path,
And boldly seized the Lamb from his jaw,
    Then scowled at the Wolf who stood in awe.
"That Lamb was unrighteously taken from me,
    'Tis mine," said the Wolf, entreatingly.
"What! Yours?" the Lion jeeringly said,
    As he tossed his mane and shook his head.
"Might makes right, else you'd not have had
    The shepherd's lamb — a meal not bad.
You know that the strong the weak oppress —
    A truth I am sure you will confess."

TREACHEROUS FRIENDSHIP.

Over hill and dale, by the Hound pursued,
   A fleet-foot Hare was at last subdued;
First the Hound would bite, as her life to take,
   Then fondle and feign amends to make.

"O that you were sincere," then said the Hare;
   "Pray show by your colors what you are
If my true friend you are, why bite so hard?
   If my enemy, why show me regard?

"Those whom we can neither trust nor distrust
   Are not true friends that treat us just;
Better the hate of an enemy,
   Than feigning friendship and base treachery."

MY LOVES.

My first was a damsel, as fair as a rose
    That blooms in the morning, fresh with dew;
She was comely; I loved her, and everyone knows
    No love like the first is so warm and so true.
I was then but a boy in my passionate teens;
    She was charming—I fondled her dearly.
Oh! I cannot forget, tho' time it me weans,
    For I loved her, yes, truly, sincerely.
Long since she has left me—lament's no avail—
    Is married—a mother—to me that is naught;
Once more on love's waves my bark I will sail—
    To grieve would be folly, with evil full fraught.

My second—a sweet little miss of thirteen—
    Had lips like twin rose-buds; and laughing gray eyes;
Resplendent as sunlight her hair's golden sheen;
    Like the ripple of brooks sweetly low her replies.
Ah! She was my idol—I worshipped her too—
    And fond were the hopes that I cherished.

I would wed her one day, my darling so true;
   Alas, furtive hopes, how they perished!
She, too, went away — I do not now care —
   Still her memory is deep in my heart —
I suppose, like my first, a mother, somewhere,
   A dear little wife doing nicely her part.

My third, and the best, the last kindled spark,
   Was a sweet little maiden, her summers sixteen,
Eyes beaming with brightness, so loving, so dark,
   And bonny brown tresses, the fairest e'er seen.
Adored I my fair one, oft my love I'd repeat,
   With a kind and affectionate heart;
I now had determined, if she beat a retreat,
   It would not be owing to my not doing my part.
I wooed and I won her — the best I must tell —
   Ever happy we've been from that day;
Life's best thing I find is the home where we dwell,
   When all help to make it pleasant to stay.

COINS.

Hope, thou art a flatterer, upright and just;
In thee life's weary pilgrims put their trust;
The poor man's hut, the mansions of the rich
Alike, with one accord, thou dost bewitch.

Base as a currency, tho' paid at court,
Thou art, O Flattery, a dernier resort;
By common custom, a coin quite often paid,
Tho' base and worthless, yet good stock in trade.

Thank God, the resurrection bone will stay
Impervious to death, and to all decay;
Fire will not burn it, nor hammer break,
Mills cannot grind it, nor water slake.

Life's wicked gayeties 'round which men cling,
First bring them pleasure, then to ruin bring;
Like the volcanic mount whose surface grows with
      flowers,
But desolate soon amid scoriac showers.

The stars are pearls of the unclouded night,
As truths are pearls of sorrow to teach the right;
And often a bitter truth, when well impressed,
Has proven useful, and its owner blest.

'Tis ease and luxury that obscures the mind,
While poverty doth its possessor grind;
But grinding sharpens —'tis a school whence
Its graduates have success immense.

We grieve as life speeds by, yet have no care,
And long each period past the new to share;
The youth longs ever to be of full age;
The business man for busiest stage;
One seeks life's honors to be known as great,
And seldom is content on time to wait;
With all regretful we all soon aspire
To gain life's rest—to be at ease, retire.

Stars! Pearls of darkness, make resplendent night;
Truths! Pearls of sorrow, teach us to know the
    right.

Beauty, thou dost with thy unerring glance
The souls of guileless men to thee entrance;
Thy art's alluring, and thou dost succeed —
An hypnotizer thou art indeed.
While yet an angel, thou hast reptile wings,
And waste thy sweetness on too many things.

Bear well misfortune with a Christian's zeal,
The world will let you bear without appeal;
The Christian fortitude so oft expressed —
Grief for their own — deeming yours a jest.

Man strives for wealth to find his trouble grows,
And strives for knowledge to find he little knows.

Contemn not men until they've injured you,
And when they have, detest and them eschew.

Of all the actions of a wise man's life,
There's none so great as to choose a wife;
His marriage mankind should the least concern,
To meddle with it most his neighbors yearn.

A hero is a soul, who, sick with ills,
Can be induced to take physicians' pills;
'Tis true they will amuse a sick man's mind
Until they kill, or nature cure will find.

'Tis well to think well, divine to act right,
But he does most who does one act contrite.

I.

THE RELATION OF MAN TO NATURE.

THE ARGUMENT.

Man is the most helpless of all beings born into this world, yet has been given control of the other beings upon the earth. Man has honor and glory, and is created without a peer.

Into the world most helpless being born,
Is Man — made like his God, earth to adorn;
Yet he, proud son of God's eternal hand,
Boasts mastery o'er the boundless sea and land;
To death, this atom, creature of the earth,
If left uncared for, doomed is he at birth;
But from his first until his final breath
Asserts o'er all the rights of life and death.
Unable what the hour shall bring and where
To tell, yet to interpret and declare
God's laws, assumes he — ways of the most high;
The heavens measures, maps out earth and sky;
Marks planets' orbits; and courses define
Of worlds — no longer human but divine!

Sport of the elements! Imperial child!
Lifeless he falls if but the air's defiled
With vapor invisible; and quakes with fear
If but the voice of thunder he doth hear.
Man, who, like the grass, to-day is glorious,
To-morrow withered, and death victorious,
Assumes to rule o'er the eternal hills;
And rivals Him who rides on clouds, and wills
The lightning's flash, the torrent's pour;
The fire-cloud's burst that warned the men of yore.
Upon the wave this raindrop takes control
Of infinite seas, where boundless billows roll.
Thus, man hath glory, splendor, honor, here,
Created Lord of Earth, without a peer!

II.

Man is a part of Nature. It is the purpose to ascertain his relation to Nature.

My theme is Nature — how 'tis linked to Man,
And Man to Nature — strange and mighty plan!
What's meant by Nature? Comprehensive term!
Nature, and super-nature, we affirm

Are often talked about, nor vain
Our efforts here to separate the twain.
To draw the line at just the limit
Of human knowledge, think not for a minute;
For no man dares to say that Nature goes
Only so far as his experience knows.
No one should be allowed to e'er contend,
Concerning things he cannot comprehend;
And say the unobserved is but a miracle,
Nor term God's mysteries empirical.
The highest knowledge still is uncontrolled,
For Nature will the strangest things unfold,
Take planets Neptune, Saturn, Mars and Jove —
Bright, shining stars, celestial worlds above:
Can sage explain the ruby hue of Mars?
Neptune's construction, that of other stars?
Is Saturn made of rock, and that bright ring
Entwined around its disk, the wondrous thing —
Is it an iron forged and made a tire
At Vulcan's smithy, kept in galling fire?
He used to work in days erstwhile, we're told,
On Ætna's height, and various things did mould.

The greatest, grandest one of his invention
Was woman, named Pandora — her I'll mention.
Yet, palaces for Mars, and for Achilles arms;
A golden chain for Juno; other charms
He made; and thunder-bolts for Jove he hurled,
That tore asunder, rent the reeling world
In desolation — made the boldest quake,
And cities crumble, as when earthquakes shake;
A wondrous smith! And from his forge and fire
Was not Saturna girded by that tire?
By Jove's high orders, then did he aspire
To whip Saturna, take his royal throne
And rule among the Gods in power alone?
Tell me, ye wise men, are these planets water,
Rock, forest, iron, gold, or other matter?
Gold, did I say? — not gold, I mean it not,
For if our sons of fair Columbia thought
Gold was, no matter where, if near or far,
In unknown worlds, or in some shining star,
They'd seek it, get it, dig it, grind it new,
And clean it, mint it, coin it, hoard it, too.

You ask me how they'd get it—please don't fret,
Stars are in mystery, undiscovered yet.
The planet Venus, distant to our view,
By telescope we see its light, 'tis true.
To tell the form or elements that make
A larger instrument than known 'twill take.
Yet Venus is a part of Nature's birth,
Like planet we inhabit, called the Earth.
By birth a part of Nature's great creation,
We may suppose it peopled by a nation.
I do not know, but such is my suggestion,
If not, what is it? That is still the question.
No one can say, with hope to be consistent,
That by a miracle the Star's existent.
For naught there is in Nature or her course,
Or in the uses of her laws and force
As supernatural, to be claimed by man;
Still, worlds are made on a mysterious plan.
Water made wine, miraculous may seem;
If 'twere not done by chemicals, I'd deem
It so. Accustomed to such changes though,
We speak of them as natural, also.

To raise one from the tomb, scarce dead a day,
Disputes the laws of life and of decay.
'Tis very strange! Not supernatural, no,
'Tis Nature's proof, and only goes to show
A higher law upon dull matter wrought
Above the limit of the things we're taught.

III.

Nature is a system of worlds, which the All-wise Father has made for the children of the Earth.

What's meant by Nature? That I'll try to tell,
Will try to please, and try to do it well.
The clustered worlds were made by God above,
That Man, his proudest creature, here might move;
Things physical, symmetrical, complex,
Organic, inorganic, be our text;
The grain of sand upon the surging shore,
The mighty waves, with loud resounding roar,
The curling vapors, darkly heaped on high —
Majestic clouds athwart the azure sky;

From microscopic atomies of life
To monsters of the deep, with terrors rife.
Gasses and solids, rocks, planets, earth and air,
All things which have a conscious being here.

IV.

Man cannot comprehend God's creation, and disobeys the laws of his Creator. He gropes his way in darkness throughout life.

Poor, foolish Man, his conscious powers obeying;
When born into this world, commences, saying:
"A mighty lord am I! Who placed me here?
I have no equal, either far or near."
Said Adam: "Do these beings rule my life?
Pray, tell me that, my own, my darling wife."
Said Eve: "Ne'er mind — I've found an apple sweet,
Come here, dear Adam, come and freely eat."
He looked and ate and was accursed then —
His sin has cursed his race of fellow-men.
What are we, then? Whence come we? Whither go?
We think, we reason, but we do not know.
Oh, wretched man! With all thy boasted powers,
Thy joys are fleeting as the summer showers;

In vain thy aspiration so sublime;
Thy fondest hopes are doomed, and, like thy time,
But speeds thee by; vainly you clasp and cling,
While Time still mocks at thee, and will thee bring
Unto the grave. All reach that bound at last —
Wrapt in oblivion, buried in the past.

V.

Man, however, belongs to the world — he is coeval with Nature and depends upon it for existence.

And how does Man to this vain world belong?
Is his a race apart from all the throng?
Man born with Nature, he must needs depend
Upon kind Nature ever to him befriend.
Man's physical constitution is the same,
Of regular organism, him I'll name.
And passions, too, the lordliest men do show
Possessed by brute creation far below.
We boast our lineage, and yet 'tis plain
Are but of clay. 'Tis useless to be vain,
For atoms of the grandest type of Man
Are seen in members of the lower clan.

The German flower-gardeners often say
That Man is only water, carbon, ammonia.
There's no abstract existence, man's first born
Ere the spiritual world he can adorn.
On earth, not freed from power of earthly bands—
So like the beast, yet lord of many lands.

VI.

Man has a common substance, which is shared by all other forms of created beings belonging to God's creation.

Organic matter? There is not one kind
In human frames, that elsewhere you'll not find.
For tissues, muscles, bones and nerves of men;
The veins, cells, carbon and the hydrogen
Are equally identical when found
As in all other forms of life abound.
The crumbled rock, the soil, the plant, the star,
Each gives to us a part of what we are.
It is no metaphor for one to say
That man who lives on earth from day to day,
Lives in the trees; lives in the leafy bowers;
Lives in the singing birds; lives in the flowers;

Lives in the rifting clouds that float on high;
Lives in the vapor of the heavenly sky.
Whether there's transmigration of the soul
There's transmigration of our bodies whole
In various other forms of life created —
For soon our bodies must be transmigrated.
We have alike a common substance given
With evil things and with things fit for heaven.
There's phosphorus in the lordliest of brains;
And iron even in a prince's veins.
And this is man — the creature called sublime,
The slave of matter, and the thrall of Time!
The Human body's born, and then it dies,
By death disintegrated where it lies.

VII.

Man is the highest type of God's creation. Science has demonstrated that there is a similarity in creation of all God's beings; and that Man has instincts and passions in common with all of them.

Proud Man takes highest place; in him we find
The loftiest order of the scale in kind;

But 'tis not difficult for us to go
From rocks to his self-conscious being, no!
For science now has clearly demonstrated —
By physiologists 'tis promulgated —
That human bodies, prior to their birth,
Go through the grades of animals of earth.
Humbling, it may be, to our human pride,
Yet 'tis a fact we cannot well deride.
In structure, Man's to animal more near
Than animal to bird, for it is clear
Man's skeleton is more like the baboon
Than skeleton of bat is like the loon.
So, too, mankind the lowest instincts share
With lower animals, as wolf or bear.
Our hands are beautiful, smooth, and wondrous fair,
Yet like the claws of lions in their lair.
In skull of wolf or hissing snake we find
A brain like that of Man, whose mighty mind
Has ruled the ages — passing strange, yet true!
From lower forms we rose to high and new.

VIII.

Natural history is incomplete without lichens, ferns, and the coral reef of the lower order of creation. It is equally so with Man, the highest type of creation.

In days of yore the ancient fancies gleam
In metamorphoses, and it would seem
The Roman Ovid, writing of to-day
In view of science, would unquestioned say:
That animals and plants in growth adorn
The brother man — a perfect being born.
Our Natural History is incomplete
If lacking lowest forms; in order meet
The lichens, ferns and mosses must be counted
Until our minds to higher forms have mounted.
As well the sponge, the coral reef, and then
It still is incomplete till we add men.
Mars may perchance be peopled, or bright Jove,
The Moon, or the bright Nebulæ world above,
With some yet strange, superior clan,
Who have no known relation to our Man.
Who think without brains, and fly without wings,

Walk without feet, without a tongue still sings.
Such beings dwell in our imagination —
To our material world have no relation.

IX.

The characteristics of Man may be perfectly described by the use of metaphors embracing the lower tribe.

The various human traits we may describe
By metaphors about the lower tribe.
We say, as fierce as lion, sly as fox,
Timid as a lamb, patient as an ox,
Busy as bees, or like the goat capricious,
Mild as a dove, like the hyena vicious.
The dog — no greater or more faithful friend —
To dwell on earth with mankind God did send;
No greater fondness shows the human mother
Than does the hen which doth her chickens hover.
For it is true in beasts we often see
What praise we most in Man, a quality
That fits the good man for the world above
Where all is gladness, peace and joyous love.

X.

Man is wholly dependent upon the lower races for subsistence, but they are not dependent upon him. There is no part of Nature but what Man makes use of. Man uses, admires, and adores Nature, and God has so made Nature that it is varied and intended to please all mankind.

While it is true that Man cannot exist
Without the lower races, they subsist;
The foxes have their holes, the birds their nest;
What has poor Man? Not where to take his rest!
From first until the final breath gives way,
These creatures minister to his wants each day;
With greater knowledge yet he scarce contrives
To live without these low, inferior lives.
That he must live, Man must breathe vital air,
Must drink from fountains, water, cool and clear,
Must feed on fruits of fields, the corn, the wheat,
The flesh of animals compelled to eat.
Man's mansion, home, to him a paradise,
He doth of wood, earth, iron, stone, devise.

Take but the natural elements away,
Man could not live upon the earth a day.
O Nature, Man doth all thy beauties love!
From atoms here to thy great works above;
He loves the beauteous landscape Nature made,
With grouping trees, and cool and grateful shade.
Music's ethereal voice which moves the soul
Is but thy air, as sweet vibrations roll
From trained voice of some great queen of song,
Or music from the woods of winged throng.
Thy works are varied for Man's pleasure here,
And Man is ever changing o'er thy sphere;
For some are never happy where are trees;
Some have no joy without the balmy breeze;
While some may love to watch meandering rills;
Some love the prairies, others love the hills;
Some love to live beside the great blue sea,
Some think it desolate as it can be.
To some philosophy and pleasure lies,
On cloudy days, amid the weeping skies.

XI.

Nature is needed to develop Man. Its influence expands his mind, and Man grows continuously in knowledge in studying the wisdom of God's creation. It teaches him the lesson of immortality.

Nature is needed to enrich Man's powers
Which God has given us as truly ours;
This world is beauteous in sights and sounds;
With Nature's myriad voices it abounds;
From rock, from river, tender flower and spray,
Come ministers of joy for every day.
Man must have Nature, with her fountains, rills,
Her prairies, lawns, her woodlands, farms, and hills,
Her birds, her beasts, her insects and her grain,
Her forests, rocks, her wonders, I maintain
Those who well know them nobler men will be,
And larger their spirituality.
O, Nature, quiet, lovely Nature, we
Under thy influence would wish to be;
To know of God's creation makes us wise;
His trees, His fruits, His plants, His flowers, His skies;
And all the universe clear-voiced shall teach,
Man mortal and decaying things must reach,

For they help teach us when this life we've trod —
Our soul immortal is — there is a God.

XII.

Man is different from the things which God created to live with him. He has power to fill God's offices here below. He controls by voluntary will. He has power of migration, and can go from pole to pole, and can live and thrive well everywhere. This is not true of God's lower creation.

Man differs from the things that God created
To live with Him; for man is separated
From mountain, forest, birds, or any beast —
O'er all creation Man is still high priest.
He has the power God's office to fulfill,
Alone controls by voluntary will;
Alone has perfect power of free migration;
Alone removes from station unto station;
On Mother Earth, changes his dwelling-place;
Alone can mingle with some other race;
Changes one air for other, east or west;
Seeks at his will the climes that he loves best;
From north to south, from forest and from plain;
Goes from the lowland to the highland main;

Or from the torrid to the frigid clime,
And lives, and likewise thrives in all, sublime.
'Tis true the dog in every clime is known,
Goes with his master, Man, from zone to zone;
The lion lives in Afric's sunny breeze,
Except when caged and carried 'cross the seas.
Seeds emigrate — that task the winds perform —
Birds fly across the ocean with the storm;
Indeed, they sometimes warmer climates seek,
At times the cooler crags and mountain peak.
But these are certainly but chance migrations,
And should not be confounded with earth's nations.
Seeds go with the winds; birds fly with the season;
God's child, proud Man, alone migrates by reason;
To no one place restricted, here to-day,
To-morrow elsewhere, as he wills or may.
By myriads each year their Emerald Isle
The Irish leave, with sad and tearful smile,
To seek a home beyond the far-off sea,
Be with his brother there forever free!
His bogs remain, and will, forever fast,
A part of Ireland, future, present, past.

The Germans come, but their black forests stay,
Enduring monuments, till Time's decay.
Man orders changes, goes where he may please
O'er all the earth, and over all the seas.
The wise man travels over seas and lands,
Notes what he wills, and thus his mind expands;
Sees many races, reads their books; and then
Learns science and the arts and tongues of men;
He thus fulfills his destiny below —
Knows well himself, and others tries to know.

XIII.

Man alone has been gifted with speech, by means of which he conveys his thoughts and expands his reason.

And then no other being but proud Man
Possesses power of speech, by which he can
Ideas express, his very thoughts convey,
Vary, enlarge, and broaden, day by day,
Nature, 'tis true, has voice; her spheres abound
With music sweet, with Nature's heavenly sound;
For there is music in the ocean's roar;
And there is music in the torrent's pour;

And there is music in the waves that crash
Upon the ocean's rocks, then roll and dash
In tide that ebbs and flows from out the sea,
With rolling sound of deepest melody.
All Nature has a voice — the insects gloat,
And sing or chirp, in their peculiar note;
The Locust's song is heard thro' all the land
To-day, as first it sang on Egypt's strand;
Chirps still the cricket at the twilight's dawn;
Croaks still the frog as in the ages gone;
The serpent hisses, rattles, warns its foes
Ere it will deal its death impending blows;
Still may be heard the cry of crocodile
Unchanged tho' centuries roll along the Nile.
The birds still twitter, scream or chirp, in talk,
Save few that do possess the power to mock;
But Man the voice of reason doth command:
His speech, his thought, his reason doth expand;
How high is he endowed — divinely wrought,
Who by his speech conveys eternal thought.

XIV.

Man can control all natural forces — can handle and tame the brute element. Man reasons and thinks for himself; invents, and by reason of his inventions, utilizes all the forces of Nature, and brings them to do his bidding.

'Tis clear that Man controls the natural forces,
Lord over mountains, valleys, water-courses,
He can the lightning harness, for his thought,
To flash around the world. And he has taught
The lower creatures to obey his will,
And all his menial duties to fulfill.
He pierces mountains, and the lakes he fills
With excavations from the stately hills;
Rivers, that in broad channels proudly go,
Are changed, in hidden million rills to flow
To houses in the cities far away,
For grateful ministry to man each day;
The deep blue ocean, with relentless waves,
Man plows his way through with great ships, and braves
Its storms and hardships, things of greatest worth
He brings from all the nations of the earth.

Forcing the elements, combining skill
To uses new, by force of power and will.
The lower beings naught invent, create,
They processes repeat, nor hesitate
For generations o'er the same to do,
Ingenious it may seem, 'tis never new.
On Syrian hills the leopards hunt to-day,
As in the ages gone they sought their prey;
The beaver builds his dam across the stream,
No more ingenious now than past, 'twould seem.
And busy bee, its cells for storing food,
Of old was just as now, tho' always good;
The ant has found no new way food to stow,
Resorting still to her old process slow.
The busy mind of man is ever wise:
He presses on, inventions to devise;
His mind, not satisfied with former deeds,
With new resources struggles and succeeds.
The rudest savage will much more invent
Than the wisest animal that God e'er sent.
The spider's web, as it doth float in air,
Can it with weavings of the loom compare?

Is the fastidious butterfly, so gay,
Flitting among the gorgeous flowers of May,
To be compared to chemist, who by skill,
Combines the flowers, their essence makes at will?

XV.

Man alone of God's created beings can interpret Nature, can read God's plan. Man has a science of Nature, even tho' it be crude, and tries to ferret out and ascertain the secrets of Nature. Even in a little flower Man finds a treasure. Animals have instinct but not reflective sense, nor Man's intelligence.

Another difference, 'tis left for Man
To interpret Nature, read God's plan.
Their law the other works of God obey,
But Man interprets well their law each day.
Back to the origin of things Man turns,
To know, explain things, quick his eyes discerns—
The past, notes changes—growths now gone will tell,
Transmits the annals of this world as well.
A century rolls and yet the raven lives,
But no account of other ravens gives.

The brute but knows its own small time and place,
It has no knowledge of its kind or race.
Man has no limit; he is not confined
To races of the past. His well-stored mind
Knows lore of former worlds; and even then
As well the present, too, for do not men
Seek knowledge of the present, past, and read
The future by the past — its teachings heed?
He cares to question Nature, ferret out
Her secrets; not content to be in doubt.
Serene forever, well content to stand
The mountain is. Careless of beast or Man
That comes or goes. It does not ask nor care,
In all its thousand years, why it is there.
The rills play down its sides; the wild goat leaps
O'er its wild crags, and 'round its rocky steeps;
It has no rival mountain, far or near,
And does not wish to know why I am here.
But Man, who dies to-morrow, tries the task
To have these questions answered, and will ask
Of all Creation's works for answer plain,
The mysteries of living to explain.

Will watch the growth of plants, still finding
    pleasure;
And in the tiniest flower a priceless treasure.
For in created things there dwells a soul —
In trees, rocks, mountains, in the streams that roll
Forever to the sea. 'Tis sweet to hear
The music of the groves. Upon the ear
The bird-notes fall but lightly — yet they bear
Soft soothing to the senses, like a prayer.
The star-sown heavens declare Creation's glory,
And Nature's varied charms repeat the story.
He sings the glories of the heavenly throng,
For him the silent stars attune their song;
And o'er the face of Nature Man will throw
Effulgent glory; 'twill in beauty glow;
He makes instructive, eloquent each part,
So wise, so skillful, so sublime his art.
Thus Man alone, how proud to bear the name,
As Nature's sole interpreter may claim.

XVI.

Man, with all his wisdom, disobeys and wilfully transgresses the laws of his creator, and is punished. He has aspirations, also, to join God in that kingdom beyond this vale of of tears, and hope for more than earthly life.

Aspiring Man! The knowledge you possess
Has also taught thee cunning, to transgress
God's laws. Of God's created things
For only Man his sinful nature brings,
To curse the world. 'Mid sin and vice he gropes,
And yet, through all, this strangest being hopes!
The star of Bethlehem to earth came down
Not to save beasts — but Man, creation's crown.
He came to save; and so, thro' storm and night,
Our timid eyes turn upward to the light.
We scan the future, not with doubt and fear,
But filled with hope of what shall yet appear.
Beyond to starry worlds, o'er time and sense,
Man leaps the boundaries to realms immense.
His ardent spirit, calm and hopeful, longs
When life is o'er to join supernal throngs.

XVII.

Man blesses God for the promise of immortal life, and hopes to be finally numbered with the just of God's creation, where he will ever praise the Giver of all. Man surely hath honor and glory here upon earth.

Almighty God! For what thy hand has given
We bless thee; Ruler of the earth and heaven.
We praise thee for immortal life, and trust
All men may yet be numbered with the just;
We thank thee, Lord, for that enduring hope,
As darkly thro' this earthly life we grope;
We worship thee, our Father, for the word
That tells thy promise Man shall be preferred.
Oh, Hope! that's long deferred, but ever still
A star, a dazzling star, that always will
Be guide of Man, poor Man upon the earth,
Doomed, fated, sad, from very hour of birth;
And when, at last, the heavenly voice shall speak
And bid thee share the endless rest ye seek,
Oh, be ye ready! ever watchful, pray!
For life's soon o'er, comes then the endless day.

Oh, holy light! Born of eternal years!
The blind shall know thee, yet rejoice in tears!
In heavenly home, beyond the starry skies,
Man yet shall praise thee, Ruler, just and wise.
Man surely hath dominion, honor, here,
Created Lord of earth, without a peer.

www.ingramcontent.com/pod-product-compliance
Lightning Source LLC
Chambersburg PA
CBHW032147230426
43672CB00011B/2479